MarcusWareing
Nutmeg & Custard

Marcus Wareing
Nutmeg & Custard

with Chantelle Nicholson

BANTAM PRESS

LONDON · TORONTO · SYDNEY · AUCKLAND · JOHANNESBURG

Lancashire-born *Marcus Wareing* began his restaurant career at The Savoy, aged just eighteen, before moving to work alongside Albert Roux at Le Gavroche. In 1993 he became sous chef at Gordon Ramsay's Aubergine restaurant and then, in 1999, with Ramsay's backing, he opened Pétrus in The Berkeley hotel in London's Knightsbridge. Pétrus won its first Michelin star within seven months of opening and went on to be awarded a second star in 2007 as well as the AA's ultimate accolade of five rosettes. Marcus also ran The Savoy Grill between 2003 and 2007, restoring it to its former glory and acheiving its first-ever Michelin star. Pétrus was relaunched as Marcus Wareing at The Berkeley in 2008 with Marcus taking over full ownership. He lives in London with his wife, Jane, and their three children, Jake, Archie and Jessie.

For my wife, Jane. Thank you for all your love and support, I could not have got this far without you, but most of all thank you for being a great mum to our very own three stars — Jake, Archie and Jessie.

TRANSWORLD PUBLISHERS
61–63 Uxbridge Road, London W5 5SA
A Random House Group Company
www.rbooks.co.uk

First published in Great Britain in 2009 by Bantam Press
an imprint of Transworld Publishers

Copyright © Marcus Wareing 2009

Marcus Wareing has asserted his right under the Copyright, Designs
and Patents Act 1988 to be identified as the author of this work.

A CIP catalogue record for this book is available from the British Library.

ISBN 9780593062111

Addresses for Random House Group Ltd companies outside the UK
can be found at: www.randomhouse.co.uk
The Random House Group Ltd Reg. No. 954009

The Random House Group Limited supports The Forest Stewardship
Council (FSC), the leading international forest-certification organization.
All our titles that are printed on Greenpeace-approved FSC-certified paper
carry the FSC logo. Our paper procurement policy can be found at
www.rbooks.co.uk/environment

Typeset in Rockwell and Scala
Design and art direction by Smith & Gilmour
Photography by Noel Murphy
Printed and bound in China by
Toppan Printing Co., (ShenZhen) Ltd.

4 6 8 10 9 7 5 3

introduction viii

weekends 2

grill room 38

orient 84

spice route 104

salad bar 122

bakery 140

puds 176

popcorn 202

ice-cream parlour 220

sweet shop 242

home larder 262

index 274

acknowledgements 279

INTRODUCTION

Nutmeg & Custard epitomizes to me the beauty of food, through ingredients and cookery. It embodies the following important ideals: flavour, texture, quality, care, technique and creativity. In this book I hope to impart these ideals to you, in order, first, to help you gain an appreciation of ingredients, and then to maximize the satisfaction you can achieve from your cookery.

My view on food and cookery is rather simple: it is about taking an ingredient and bringing out the best in it by flavour combinations and cookery techniques. Take a nutmeg, for example; it looks like a small brown ball, yet holds a unique taste and aroma that can be captured and enhanced by other ingredients. This is what I want to share.

'Why *Nutmeg & Custard*?' you may ask. 'Is this a pastry book?' No, just two of my favourite foods, which together create something magical. A perfect custard is comforting – warm, sweet and silky. Nutmeg is the extra something special that takes it to another level. My grandma used to make the perfect baked egg custard tart with crisp, buttery pastry. My mother could never get the pastry right, though, so she baked egg custard in an earthenware dish and it was the ultimate in comfort and flavour. The scent of nutmeg thus evokes memories of my childhood and family.

I have replicated these childhood ideals in this book, in chapters such as 'Sweet Shop' and 'Ice-Cream Parlour' – old favourites taken to a new, more modern level for you and your family to enjoy both creating and tasting.

WEEKENDS

Weekends at home to me are all about spending time with my family. I think a cooked breakfast, for all to share, is a great way to start off the weekend. Give the Home-made Crumpets with Burnt Honey Butter (page 6) a try; there is something really satisfying and slightly novel about making something that you normally buy from the supermarket. Also, the Chorizo-stuffed French Toast with Manchego (page 17) is perfect champagne-breakfast fare – I am sure your friends can't wait to be invited!

Given that I am also a bit of a home-body, I love a winter's night in, with a comfort-inducing dinner in front of the fire – try the Cannelloni with Spinach, Pumpkin and Nutmeg (page 18) for a delicious meal that is best if prepared a day or two in advance (a handy thing to prepare during the week to maximize time at the weekend).

Also try the Bacon Roly-polies (page 24) and Herbed Sausage Rolls (page 12), which are great as a snack with an ice-cold beer. Both can be frozen and defrosted as and when you don't have time to cook.

4

Corn custards

MAKES 4

400g frozen or tinned and drained
    sweetcorn kernels
200ml semi-skimmed or whole milk
2 medium free-range eggs
100g crème fraîche
½ tsp table salt
coarsely ground black pepper
1 whole nutmeg

1 Preheat the oven to 130°C/250°F/gas mark ½.

2 Place the sweetcorn in a saucepan with half the milk and bring to a gentle simmer until soft. Blend until smooth.

3 Add the remaining milk, eggs, crème fraîche, salt and pepper and whisk to combine.

4 Divide the mixture between four buttered ramekins and liberally grate the nutmeg over the top.

5 Place the ramekins on a tray in the oven for 20 minutes until just wobbly in the centre. Leave to rest for 5 minutes before serving with toasted crusty bread for a Sunday night dinner.

1 In one bowl mix the flour, baking powder and seasoning together. Put the butter into a small saucepan and melt over a moderate heat. In a separate bowl, whisk the eggs with the melted butter, sweetcorn and coriander. Gently fold the wet mixture into the dry mixture, making sure you don't over-mix. Set aside.

2 Mix the crème fraîche, chilli sauce, lime juice and seasoning together and gently fold in the avocado.

3 Heat a frying pan over a moderate heat, add the honey to caramelize, then toss the Parma ham lightly in the caramel for 1 minute. Remove from the pan and set aside.

4 Heat 1 tbsp of the vegetable oil in a medium-sized frying pan over a moderate to high heat. When hot, drop tablespoonfuls of the fritter mixture into the hot pan and cook each side until golden and cooked through. Add more oil to the pan for each batch of fritters you cook. Serve immediately, topped with the Parma ham and the avocado mixture.

5

Sweetcorn fritters with avocado and caramelized parma ham

SERVES 4–6

FRITTERS
100g plain flour
1 tsp baking powder
½ tsp table salt
½ tsp coarsely ground black pepper
50g unsalted butter
2 medium free-range eggs
450g frozen and defrosted or tinned
    and drained sweetcorn kernels
¼ bunch coriander, leaves chopped

AVOCADO
1 tbsp crème fraîche
½ tsp sweet chilli sauce
juice of half a lime
½ tsp table salt
½ tsp coarsely ground black pepper
1 ripe avocado, peeled, stoned and diced

PARMA HAM
1 tbsp clear honey
8 slices Parma ham

3 tbsp vegetable oil

6

Home-made crumpets with burnt honey butter

MAKES 6

CRUMPETS
250ml semi-skimmed
   or whole milk
200g plain flour
1 tsp fast-action dried yeast
1 tsp caster or granulated sugar
½ tsp table salt

BURNT HONEY BUTTER
5 tbsp clear honey
125g unsalted butter,
   at room temperature
½ tsp Maldon sea salt

2 tbsp vegetable oil

1 Mix together all the ingredients for the crumpets in a bowl, cover and leave in a warm place to double in volume for 20 minutes. Whilst proving, make the butter.

2 Place the honey in a small saucepan over a moderate to high heat. Allow to bubble until a deep golden colour is reached, then remove from the heat and allow to cool.

3 Beat the butter until fluffy and pale, add the salt, then fold in the honey. Put the bowl in the fridge.

4 When the crumpet dough has doubled in volume, put a large frying pan over a moderate heat, add 1 tbsp of the vegetable oil and place three greased egg rings in the pan.

5 Spoon the crumpet mixture into the rings until two thirds full. Allow the undersides to cook slowly until the mixture has set and the bubbles on top have burst. Repeat with the remaining oil and mixture, then serve with the butter.

1 Put the bacon into a large saucepan over a moderate heat and allow the fat to render and the bacon to cook.

2 Add the onion, garlic, thyme and paprika, and cook until golden. Add the remaining ingredients and simmer gently for 10 minutes.

3 Turn off the heat, cover and allow to sit for a couple of hours for the flavour to develop. Before serving, remove the thyme and heat through until simmering.

8

Smoky baked beans

SERVES 4

100g smoked bacon, diced into
    small pieces
1 medium onion, peeled and diced
2 cloves garlic, peeled and crushed
¼ bunch thyme
1 tsp smoked paprika
1 × 400g tin white beans
    (haricots blancs)
1 × 400g tin red kidney beans
1 tbsp soft brown sugar
1 tsp black treacle
2 tbsp tomato purée
125g tomato passata
½ tsp table salt
coarsely ground black pepper

Smashed plum tomato bruschetta with poached eggs

SERVES 4

8 large, ripe plum tomatoes, diced
2 cloves garlic, peeled and crushed
¼ bunch thyme leaves
½ tsp table salt
1 tsp caster or granulated sugar
4 tbsp extra-virgin olive oil
4 slices pain de campagne
    or sourdough bread
Maldon sea salt
1 tsp vinegar
4 large free-range eggs
coarsely ground black pepper
½ bunch basil, leaves chopped

1 Place the tomatoes, garlic, thyme, salt and sugar in a small saucepan over a moderate heat and allow to simmer gently.

2 Meanwhile, heat a large griddle pan until hot. Oil each side of the slices of bread and sprinkle them with sea salt. Grill each side of the bread until well coloured, then set aside and keep warm until the eggs are ready.

3 Heat a deep pan of seasoned water and the vinegar until gently simmering. Break the eggs into individual cups or ramekins, whisk the water, then gently pour the eggs in, ensuring the water is still swirling.

4 When the whites are set, remove the eggs with a slotted spoon and place them on paper towels. Sprinkle with sea salt and a generous grinding of pepper.

5 Stir the basil into the tomato mixture, then divide between the four slices of toast and top each with a poached egg. Serve immediately.

Porridge with maple bananas and greek yogurt

SERVES 4

50g jumbo rolled oats
50g porridge oats
½ tsp table salt
1 tsp ground cinnamon
250ml semi-skimmed
    or whole milk
250ml water
1 tbsp unsalted butter
2 very ripe bananas, each
    cut into 6 slices
8 tbsp maple syrup
300g thick Greek yogurt,
    to serve

1 Place the oats, salt, cinnamon, milk and water in a medium-sized saucepan over a low to moderate heat, stirring regularly, for 5–10 minutes.

2 Heat the butter in a medium-sized frying pan over a high heat, add the banana slices and brown them slightly on each side. Add the maple syrup, then remove from the heat.

3 When the oats are cooked and have soaked up most of the liquid, divide the porridge between four serving bowls. Place three slices of banana and a large dollop of Greek yogurt on each. Serve immediately.

Herbed sausage rolls

MAKES 6 LARGE OR 18 SMALL ROLLS

FILLING
1 large potato, peeled and diced
500g sausagemeat
500g pork mince
¼ bunch thyme leaves
¼ bunch parsley, chopped
¼ bunch sage, chopped
1 medium onion, peeled and diced
3 tbsp tomato ketchup
3 tbsp brown sauce
1 tsp tomato purée
1 tsp soy sauce
1 tsp Worcestershire sauce

3 rolls pre-rolled puff pastry
2 medium free-range egg yolks,
    lightly beaten
Maldon sea salt

1 Preheat the oven to 180°C/350°F/gas mark 4. Put the potato in seasoned cold water and bring to a gentle simmer until soft, then strain under running water until cool.

2 Combine the cooked potato with the rest of the ingredients for the filling in a bowl and mix well.

3 Lay one pastry sheet on your work surface. Spread a third of the sausage mixture evenly on to two thirds of the pastry.

4 Brush the remaining third of the pastry with egg yolk, then roll the pastry over to form a cylinder. Repeat with the remaining pastry sheets and sausage mixture.

5 Wrap each roll in clingfilm and put in the freezer for 10 minutes, then remove and brush each roll with egg yolk and sprinkle with sea salt.

6 Using a very sharp knife, carefully slice the rolls into the desired size. Lay them on a baking tray lined with baking paper and bake for 15–20 minutes until golden.

1 Put the barley in a saucepan of lightly salted cold water and bring to the boil. When it has partly cooked (still quite firm to the bite in the centre – after about 10 minutes), remove from the heat and strain.

2 Put the barley in a clean saucepan with the salt and, over a low heat, ladle in the stock little by little as the barley absorbs it.

3 When the barley is al dente, mix in the butter, the mascarpone, then the herbs and Parmesan. Season to taste and serve immediately.

14

Herbed barley risotto

SERVES 2-4

150g pearl barley
½ tsp table salt
200ml beef stock
200ml chicken stock
50g unsalted butter, diced
100g mascarpone
¼ bunch tarragon, leaves chopped
¼ bunch chives, chopped
¼ bunch parsley, leaves chopped
50g Parmesan, grated
coarsely ground black pepper

'Friday night in' platter

SERVES 4–6

CROSTINI
1 baguette, thinly sliced
extra-virgin olive oil
Maldon sea salt

SUNBLUSH TOMATO
AND ROCKET PESTO
200g sunblush tomatoes
100ml oil from the tomatoes
1 clove garlic, peeled and crushed
50g Parmesan, grated
100g rocket
50g pine nuts, toasted
½ tsp table salt

PARMA HAM AND
MOZZARELLA BITES
8 baby mozzarella balls
8 basil leaves
4 slices Parma ham, halved lengthways
vegetable oil

GARLIC AND HERB
MUSHROOMS
2 tbsp vegetable oil
200g button mushrooms, halved
2 cloves garlic, peeled and crushed
1 tbsp thyme leaves
1 tbsp parsley, leaves chopped
salt and coarsely ground black pepper
25g unsalted butter

BABY PLUM TOMATO, AVOCADO
AND CORIANDER SALSA
1 × 250g punnet baby plum tomatoes,
    quartered
1 avocado, peeled, stoned and diced
½ bunch coriander, leaves chopped
½ red onion, peeled and finely diced
4 tbsp sweet chilli sauce
juice of half a lime
salt and coarsely ground black pepper

1 For the crostini, preheat the oven to 180°C/350°F/gas mark 4. Arrange the slices of baguette on a baking tray, drizzle with olive oil and sprinkle with sea salt. Bake for 5–8 minutes or until lightly golden and crispy.

2 For the pesto, blend all the ingredients together in a blender or using a stick blender. Adjust the seasoning if necessary.

3 For the bites, wrap the basil around the mozzarella, then the Parma ham around both. Secure with a toothpick. Before serving, heat a little vegetable oil in a frying pan and lightly fry the balls until just coloured. Drain and serve immediately.

4 For the mushrooms, heat the oil in a large frying pan over a moderate heat. Add the remaining ingredients, except for the butter, and fry until everything begins to colour. Add the butter and allow to cook a little further, then remove from the heat and keep warm.

5 For the salsa, combine all the ingredients, folding gently so that the avocado doesn't break up. Adjust the seasoning to taste.

6 Arrange all the items on a large platter with a selection of your favourite cheeses, olives and bread.

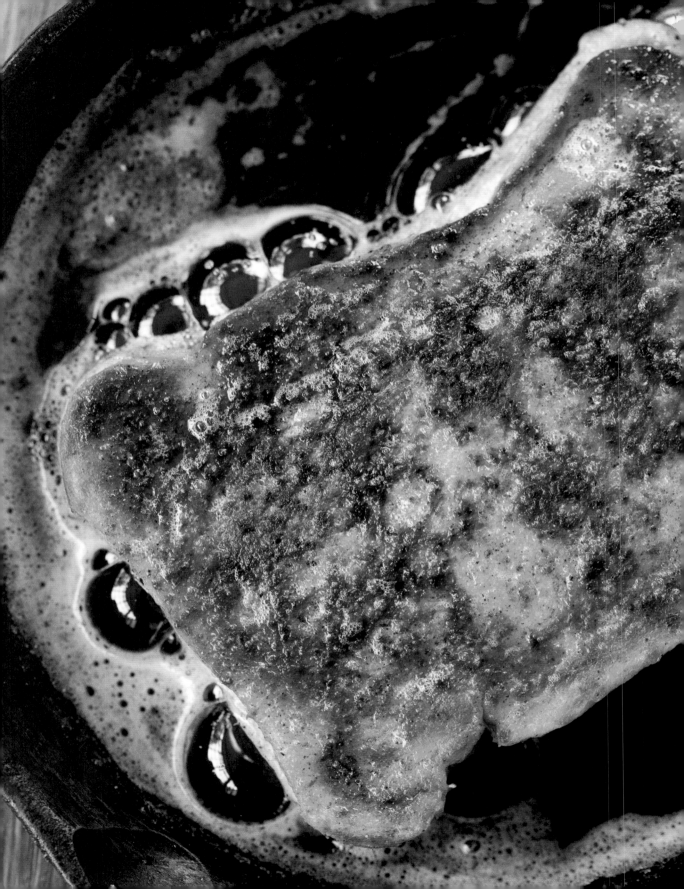

Chorizo-stuffed french toast with manchego

SERVES 4

5 tbsp vegetable oil
1 medium onion, peeled and
   finely diced
100g chorizo, peeled and diced
50g Manchego cheese, grated
pinch table salt
coarsely ground black pepper
1 loaf of your favourite bread,
   cut into 8 slices (2cm thick)
3 medium free-range eggs, beaten
300ml semi-skimmed or
   whole milk
½ tsp smoked paprika
50g unsalted butter

1 Heat 1 tbsp of the vegetable oil in a medium-sized frying pan over a moderate heat. Cook the onion and chorizo until soft, then mix with the cheese, salt and pepper to taste.

2 Divide the mixture between four of the slices of bread, leaving a 1cm edge on each piece. In a large bowl gently beat the eggs and milk together. Brush the edges of bread with a little of the beaten egg mixture, then place the other slices of bread on top to make sandwiches and press down to seal.

3 Heat another tablespoon of the vegetable oil in a large frying pan over a moderate heat.

4 Place one of the sandwiches in the egg mixture and allow to soak for 30 seconds, then turn over and soak the other side. Dust with the smoked paprika, then put in the pan.

5 Repeat the egg-soaking with another sandwich. Meanwhile, brown the first sandwich on each side, then add a quarter of the butter and brown further.

6 Remove the sandwich, clean the pan and repeat the process with the remaining three sandwiches. Serve warm, with a dollop of crème fraîche if desired.

Cannelloni with spinach, pumpkin and nutmeg

SERVES 4

¼ large pumpkin or butternut
  squash (approximately 700g),
  peeled and diced
2 tbsp vegetable oil
500g spinach
600ml semi-skimmed
  or whole milk
2 bay leaves
½ tsp table salt
½ medium onion, peeled
1 clove garlic, peeled
6 whole cloves
25g unsalted butter
3 tbsp plain flour
200g cream cheese
2 nutmegs, freshly grated
⅔ 250g packet dried
  cannelloni tubes
1 tsp vegetable oil
½ medium onion, peeled
  and finely diced
2 cloves garlic, peeled
2 tbsp balsamic vinegar
500g sieved tomato passata
4 tbsp tomato purée
1 tbsp sugar
¼ bunch thyme
½ tsp table salt
½ tsp coarsely ground black pepper

100g grated Emmental cheese
125g pumpkin seeds, toasted

1 Preheat the oven to 180°C/350°F/gas mark 4. Toss the pumpkin in the vegetable oil and season, then place on a roasting tray and bake for 20–25 minutes or until golden. Mash with a potato masher or fork, season to taste and set aside.

2 Bring a large pan of salted water to the boil. Add the spinach for 30 seconds, then transfer to a colander sitting in iced water. When cool, squeeze the spinach to remove excess water and chop into small pieces.

3 Put the milk, bay leaves and salt in a medium-sized saucepan. Stud the onion and garlic with the cloves and add to the pan. Heat very gently for 10 minutes to allow the flavours to infuse, then remove the bay leaves, onion and garlic.

4 In another saucepan melt the butter, then add the flour and mix well. Slowly pour in the hot milk, whisking well. Cook over a low heat until it has thickened (although it will be runnier than you are used to) and adjust the seasoning if required.

5 Mix the spinach with the cream cheese and nutmeg and season to taste. Using a piping bag or a teaspoon, stuff the cannelloni tubes vertically with the pumpkin mash in the bottom half of each tube and the spinach mixture in the top half.

6 In a medium-sized pan, heat the tablespoon of oil and brown the onion and garlic. Deglaze the pan with the vinegar, add the remaining ingredients and simmer for 5 minutes.

7 Line up the tubes in an appropriate-sized baking dish and pour the tomato sauce over them. Top with the white sauce, Emmental cheese and pumpkin seeds, and bake in the oven for 45–60 minutes or until the pasta is al dente.

Baked eggs with pancetta and rye bread soldiers

SERVES 4

8 thin slices rye bread
2 tbsp unsalted butter, softened
8 slices pancetta
2 tbsp olive oil
50g unsalted butter
juice of half a lemon
½ tsp table salt
½ tsp coarsely ground black pepper
4 large free-range eggs

1 Preheat the oven to 180°C/350°F/gas mark 4. Spread each slice of bread with butter and lay two slices of pancetta on each of four of the slices of bread. Place the other pieces of rye bread on top and flatten with a rolling pin.

2 Butter the outside of the sandwiches, then cut each one into 6–8 soldiers. Drizzle the olive oil on an oven tray and place the soldiers on it. Bake for 4 minutes, flip them over, then bake for a further 4 minutes, until crispy.

3 Turn the oven down to 165°C/325°F/gas mark 3. Melt the butter in a saucepan over a moderate heat, whisking until it turns golden brown and gives off a nutty smell. Remove from the heat and whisk in the lemon juice, salt and pepper.

4 Divide the butter between four ovenproof ramekins and crack an egg into each one. Place the ramekins in a roasting tin one quarter filled with hot water.

5 Carefully place in the oven and bake for 6–8 minutes until the eggs are only wobbly in the centre. Remove and serve immediately, accompanied by the soldiers.

Baked camembert with walnut and mushroom fricassee

SERVES 2–4

1 × 250g wheel mature Camembert
    (or other soft cheese of your choice)
2 tbsp unsalted butter
50g walnuts, roughly chopped
1 clove garlic, peeled and crushed
200g mixed seasonal mushrooms
¼ tsp table salt
1 tbsp Madeira wine
¼ bunch flat-leaf parsley,
    leaves chopped
1 tbsp truffle oil (optional)
coarsely ground black pepper

1 Preheat oven to 165°C/325°F/gas mark 3. Place the cheese in a small ovenproof dish and bake for 10 minutes.

2 Meanwhile, heat 1 tbsp of the butter in a medium-sized frying pan. When foaming, add the walnuts. Stir constantly until the nuts have browned, then remove them from the pan.

3 In a clean frying pan, heat the remaining tablespoon of butter. When foaming, add the garlic, mushrooms and salt, and cook until lightly golden. Add the Madeira and shake the pan well. Add the parsley, stir well, then remove from the heat.

4 Stir in the walnuts and spoon the mixture over the warm cheese. Drizzle the truffle oil (if using) over the cheese and season with black pepper. Serve with your favourite fresh bread.

Bacon roly-polies

MAKES 12–15

250g plain flour, plus a little extra
    for dusting
3 tsp baking powder
½ tsp table salt
75g unsalted butter, diced and
    cold, plus another 25g
200–250ml semi-skimmed
    or whole milk
8 large rashers shoulder or back
    bacon, rind removed
1 medium onion, peeled and
    finely chopped
100g cream cheese
100g Cheddar cheese, grated
½ bunch flat-leaf parsley, chopped
1 clove garlic, peeled and crushed

1 Preheat the oven to 180°C/350°F/gas mark 4.

2 Place the flour, baking powder and salt in a large bowl, then rub in the cold, diced butter using your hands.

3 Add the milk gradually, while mixing, until just combined. Turn out the dough on to a floured surface and roll into a rectangle 1cm thick.

4 Melt the remaining butter in a small saucepan over a moderate heat. Brush the dough with some of the melted butter, then layer the bacon on top, leaving a 2cm edge on one of the long sides of the dough.

5 Mix the onion, cheeses, parsley and garlic together and spread evenly over the bacon.

6 Brush the bare edge of the dough with water, then roll into a spiral, sealing the edge brushed with water to the body of the roll. Wrap the roll in clingfilm and refrigerate for 20 minutes.

7 Cut the roll into slices and place, spiral side up, on a baking tray lined with baking paper. Bake for 15 minutes or until golden.

26

Moroccan-spiced stuffed kabocha squash

SERVES 4

1 medium kabocha squash
1 tbsp cumin seeds
½ tsp ground cinnamon
1 cardamom pod, crushed
100g couscous
50g dates, stoned and chopped
150g cooked chickpeas, strained
50g toasted pine nuts
1 tsp table salt
250ml chicken or vegetable stock,
    plus a little extra if necessary
¼ bunch coriander, chopped

1 Preheat the oven to 180°C/350°F/gas mark 4.

2 Slice the top 3cm off the kabocha squash and reserve. Thoroughly scoop out the seeds with a spoon and discard.

3 Place the spices in a small frying pan and dry-fry until fragrant. Crush with a pestle and mortar, then mix with the couscous, dates, chickpeas, pine nuts and salt.

4 Spoon the couscous into the squash cavity while you are bringing the stock to the boil. Once it has reached boiling point, pour it carefully into the squash cavity and mix well with the couscous.

5 Place the top back on the squash and put it in a roasting tin in the oven. Bake for 30 minutes, then take it out of the oven and check if you need to add more stock to the couscous. Continue baking for a further 30 minutes, then check the tenderness of both the squash and the couscous.

6 To serve, slice the squash into wedges and serve garnished with the chopped coriander, accompanied by tamarind or mango chutney and thick Greek yogurt.

Roast pumpkin, courgette and piquillo pepper pesto lasagne

SERVES 4–6

½ small pumpkin
    (approximately 800g)
3 tbsp vegetable oil
2 courgettes, sliced diagonally
    into ½cm-thick slices
1 medium onion, peeled and diced
1 clove garlic, peeled and crushed
6 Piquillo peppers, finely sliced
2 tbsp balsamic vinegar
50g Parmesan, grated
50g pumpkin seeds, toasted
2 tbsp extra-virgin olive oil
100g Cheddar cheese, grated
6 tbsp mascarpone
salt and coarsely ground black pepper
6 sheets dried lasagne
4 tbsp pumpkin seeds, toasted

1 Preheat the oven to 180°C/350°F/gas mark 4.

2 Peel the pumpkin and chop the flesh into chunks. Lay them in a roasting tin and coat in 1 tbsp of the vegetable oil. Season well and place in the oven for 20–30 minutes until a dark golden brown. Remove and allow to cool.

3 Heat a griddle pan until smoking, brush the courgette strips with another tablespoon of the oil, season well, then grill quickly on each side.

4 Heat the last tablespoon of vegetable oil in a saucepan and add the onion, garlic and peppers. Sweat down until soft, then add the vinegar and cook until syrupy.

5 Allow to cool for 20 minutes, then blitz together with the Parmesan, pumpkin seeds and olive oil.

6 Mix 75g of the Cheddar cheese with the mascarpone and a generous amount of black pepper. Set aside.

7 Bring a large pan of salted water to the boil. Add the lasagne sheets for 30 seconds, then place them in iced water. When completely cool, remove and lay them on paper towels.

8 In a baking dish, layer the pumpkin, courgettes, mascarpone mixture and pesto between the sheets of pasta. Finish with a sheet of pasta, then sprinkle with the remaining Cheddar cheese, pumpkin seeds and more black pepper. Bake for 25 minutes or until bubbling.

Sweetcorn velouté with chorizo foam

SERVES 6-8

SWEETCORN VELOUTÉ
1 tbsp vegetable oil
4 cobs of sweetcorn, kernels
    and cobs separated
1 litre chicken or vegetable stock
¼ bunch thyme
25g unsalted butter
½ tsp table salt
500ml whole milk
CHORIZO FOAM
100g chorizo, diced
100ml semi-skimmed
    or whole milk
50ml single cream

1 Heat the vegetable oil in a large saucepan. When hot, add the corn cobs and brown all over. Add the chicken stock and thyme and boil gently for 20 minutes. Strain through a fine sieve and set aside.

2 Meanwhile, heat a small frying pan, add the chorizo and cook for 5 minutes. Add the milk and cream, heat gently, then remove from the heat.

3 Blend and pass through a fine sieve, adjusting the seasoning if necessary. Refrigerate immediately.

4 For the soup, heat the butter in a medium to large saucepan. Add the corn kernels and salt, then cook gently for 5 minutes.

5 Add the milk and the corn stock made earlier, and allow to simmer gently for 10 minutes. Blend well, then pass through a fine sieve. Taste and adjust the seasoning if necessary.

6 To serve, pour the chilled chorizo foam into a cream whipper. Secure the lid tightly, then inject one gas charge. Shake and test that the foam is holding up; if not, shake a little more and try again.

7 Pour the hot soup into six or eight serving glasses, then top with the chilled foam.

Pan-fried mackerel, chorizo-braised leeks and shallot crisps

SERVES 4

250ml vegetable oil, plus
    an extra 1 tbsp
2 banana shallots, peeled
    and sliced
1 tbsp plain flour
1½ tsp table salt
25g unsalted butter
1 large leek, white part only,
    sliced into 1cm-thick slices
100g chorizo, diced
½ tsp smoked paprika
3 tbsp chicken stock
4 fillets mackerel, pin-boned,
    skinned and scored

1 Put the 250ml vegetable oil in a small saucepan over a moderate heat. When it reaches 140°C, place the shallot rings in the flour and coat quickly, then drop into the hot oil and fry until golden. Remove with a slotted spoon and place on paper towels. Season with a ½ tsp of the salt and set aside.

2 Heat the butter in a medium-sized, deep frying pan over a moderate heat. Add the leeks with another ½ tsp of the salt and brown lightly. Add the chorizo and paprika and cook for 5 minutes, then add the stock and simmer gently for a further few minutes.

3 Put the 1 tbsp vegetable oil in a non-stick frying pan over a moderate heat. When hot, season the mackerel with the remaining ½ tsp salt and place skin side down in the frying pan. Cook until golden, then remove the pan from the heat and turn the fish over for 1 minute. Serve immediately, with the leeks underneath and the crispy shallots on top.

Pot roast quails with lentils and winter vegetables

SERVES 4

5 tbsp vegetable oil
4 quails

MIREPOIX
¼ bunch thyme
2 bay leaves
4 cloves garlic, halved
1 onion, peeled and quartered
2 star anise
8 white peppercorns
½ tsp toasted cumin seeds
1 carrot, peeled and quartered

100ml white wine
500ml chicken or vegetable stock
2 parsnips, peeled and cut
   into wedges
1 small swede, peeled and
   cut into wedges
2 carrots, peeled and cut
   into wedges
100g puy lentils, soaked in
   water for 2 hours
½ tsp table salt

1 Heat 4 tbsp of the vegetable oil in a large casserole with a lid. Season the quails all over, then add to the hot oil and brown evenly. Remove and set aside.

2 Add the *mirepoix* ingredients to the same pan and cook until browned. Add the white wine and reduce to a syrup, then add the stock and bring to a simmer. Strain the liquid and reserve.

3 Heat the remaining vegetable oil in the pan and brown the parsnip, swede and carrot. Add the reserved stock, the lentils, the salt and the quails and simmer gently for 15 minutes with the lid on. Sprinkle with the chopped parsley and serve immediately.

Bacon, lettuce, tomato and avocado salsa loaf

SERVES 4

1 large focaccia or ciabatta loaf,
    sliced in half lengthways
4 tbsp extra-virgin olive oil

AIOLI
1 medium free-range egg
1 tsp English mustard
1 tsp white wine vinegar
½ tsp table salt
1 clove garlic, peeled and crushed
200ml vegetable oil

SALSA
4 ripe plum tomatoes, diced
½ tsp table salt
1 tbsp sweet chilli sauce
juice of half a lemon
½ tsp coarsely ground black pepper
2 ripe avocados, peeled, stoned
    and diced
¼ bunch coriander, leaves chopped

8 rashers streaky bacon
1 iceberg lettuce, washed and
    leaves separated

1 Preheat the oven to 200°C/400°F/gas mark 6.

2 Heat a griddle pan over a moderate heat. Oil the bread and chargrill until crispy on the underside. Set aside.

3 Make the aioli by whisking the egg, mustard, vinegar, salt and garlic together, then slowly whisking in the oil.

4 For the salsa, mix together the tomatoes, salt, sweet chilli, lemon juice and pepper, then gently fold in the avocado and the coriander.

5 Place the bacon on a baking tray and bake in the oven until crispy.

6 Place the bread in the oven for a couple of minutes to warm through, then spread each piece with the aioli.

7 Lay the bacon on the bottom slice of bread followed by the salsa and lettuce. Place the lid of the bread on top and slice into four pieces. Serve while warm.

Poached and roasted chicken with almond and thyme crust and chargrilled cauliflower

SERVES 4

POACHING STOCK
1 carrot, peeled and halved
1 onion, peeled and halved
1 stalk celery, halved
¼ bunch thyme
¼ bunch tarragon
4 cloves garlic, halved
6 black peppercorns
½ tsp table salt

CHICKEN
1 medium free-range corn-fed
    chicken
1 tsp wholegrain mustard
100ml double cream
¼ bunch tarragon, leaves chopped

CRUST
100g almonds, skin on, toasted
200g dense brown bread,
    crusts removed
50g Parmesan, grated
½ bunch thyme leaves
½ tsp table salt
4 tbsp olive oil

CAULIFLOWER
1 cauliflower, cut into large florets
1 tbsp vegetable oil
½ tsp table salt
½ tsp curry powder
50g Macadamia nuts, toasted
    and finely chopped
¼ bunch flat-leaf parsley,
    leaves chopped

1 Place the ingredients for the poaching stock into a large saucepan and cover with warm water. Bring to a gentle simmer, then add the chicken, topping up with more water if necessary. Cover with a lid and simmer very gently for 40 minutes.

2 Remove the chicken from the stock and allow to dry off slightly. Strain the stock into a clean saucepan, bring to the boil and continue to boil gently until it has reduced to a third. Remove the pan from the heat and whisk in the mustard and cream.

3 Preheat the oven to 150°C/300°F/gas mark 2. Make the crust by putting all the ingredients into a food processor and whizzing until it clumps together. Press the crust on to the chicken, then place it in the oven for 45 minutes.

4 For the cauliflower, put a chargrill pan over a very high heat. Blanch the cauliflower for 3 minutes in seasoned water, then drain. Toss the florets in the vegetable oil and salt, then chargrill. Sprinkle with the curry powder when grilled.

5 When ready to serve, reheat the sauce gently and whisk in the chopped tarragon. Sprinkle the Macadamias and parsley over the cauliflower and serve.

GRILL ROOM

The Grill Room encompasses robust and flavoursome food. Traditionally the rooms themselves are grand affairs, full of character and with a masculine undertone. However, I think of a modern grill room as plush, cosy and bustling. To match this you need great food, good wine and good company.

The history of The Savoy Grill enchants and excites. It used to have that feeling for me even when I was an eighteen-year-old trainee just beginning my career. It was such a fulfilling pleasure to be able to restore it to its former glory in later years, when I went on to run it as Marcus Wareing at The Savoy Grill. Historically, trolleys were used in the room to convey a sense of grandeur and theatre – an idea that I recreated, including a smoked and cured salmon trolley, a cheese trolley and a fantastic dessert trolley at lunchtime. The skills possessed by the front-of-house team in the Grill's heyday were incredible; they could carve a grouse at the table with surgeon-like precision and speed, or take a Dover sole off the bone in one fluid motion. It really was an experience, even before the food reached the plate.

The dishes in this chapter capture a little of the soul of a grill room in their robustness – so do as above, and enjoy them with good wine and good company.

Tomato, cumin and saffron braised lamb neck

SERVES 4–6

4 tbsp vegetable oil
6 lamb neck fillets
½ tsp table salt
1 bulb garlic, halved lengthways
1 large onion, peeled and halved
1 carrot, peeled and cut into four
1 stalk celery, halved
1 leek, white part only, halved
4 plum tomatoes, quartered
2 tbsp tomato purée
250ml white wine
1 litre chicken stock
1 litre beef stock
2 tbsp cumin seeds, dry toasted
¼ bunch thyme
¼ bunch coriander
4 pinches saffron

1 Heat the oil in a large saucepan over a moderate to high heat. Season the lamb necks well, then place in the hot oil and brown all over. Remove and set aside.

2 Put the garlic, onion, carrot, celery and leek into the pan and brown well. Add the tomatoes, tomato purée and wine, and reduce to a syrup, stirring occasionally.

3 Add the stock, cumin seeds, herbs and saffron, and the lamb necks. Allow to simmer very gently with a lid on for 3–4 hours until the lamb is tender.

4 When tender, remove the lamb gently from the liquid and leave to cool. Strain the cooking juices into a clean saucepan, bring to a gentle simmer and reduce to a thick sauce. Slice the lamb and serve with the sauce.

Smoky pulled pork butties

SERVES 4–6

MARINADE
1 tsp smoked paprika
4 tbsp black treacle
4 tbsp clear honey
½ nutmeg, freshly grated
½ tsp ground mace
1 medium red chilli, finely chopped
2 tbsp tomato purée
100ml soy sauce
½ tsp ground cumin

PORK
1 pork shoulder, boned
   (approximately 1.2kg)
½ bunch thyme
1 tbsp black mustard seeds
2 bay leaves
½ bulb garlic, halved lengthways
200ml malt vinegar
chicken stock, vegetable stock
   or water to cover

1 Combine the ingredients for the marinade and smother over the pork shoulder. Cover, refrigerate and allow to marinate overnight.

2 The following day, place the shoulder, with all the excess marinade, into a saucepan or casserole so that it fits snugly. Add the herbs, garlic and vinegar, and top up with water, or chicken or vegetable stock. Cover and place on a low heat so that the liquid is only just simmering. Allow to cook slowly for 4–6 hours until very tender.

3 Light your barbecue and get the coals smouldering. Gently remove the pork from the liquid and place it on a small, foil-lined tray. Strain the liquid and place back on a moderate heat to simmer rapidly and reduce.

4 Put the tray with the pork on the top rack of the barbecue and cover the entire barbecue with the lid or foil (there should not be any flames on the coals – they should merely be smoking). Allow the pork to smoke for 10 minutes, then remove and brush all over with the reduced cooking liquid.

5 Return the pork to the barbecue, re-cover the barbecue and allow the meat to smoke for a further 10 minutes. Remove and shred with two forks. Serve immediately with thick, crusty white bread.

Sticky sesame pork ribs

SERVES 4

MARINADE
4 tbsp sesame oil
8 tbsp soy sauce
4 tbsp clear honey
2 tbsp golden syrup
3 tbsp peanut butter
juice of 1 orange
2 cloves garlic, peeled
  and crushed
2 tbsp sweet chilli sauce
75g fresh root ginger, peeled
  and finely grated
1 tsp Chinese 5-spice powder

12 large pork ribs
2 tbsp vegetable oil
2 tbsp sesame seeds

1 Combine the ingredients for the marinade and mix well. Smother the ribs in it, cover and refrigerate for a minimum of 6 hours, or preferably overnight.

2 Preheat the oven to 190°C/375°F/gas mark 5. Put the vegetable oil in a large roasting tin and place it in the oven to heat for 5 minutes, then add the ribs. Return to the oven for 20 minutes, turning after 10 minutes.

3 Add the sesame seeds, then bake for a further 3–4 minutes until they have turned golden. Remove from the oven and allow to rest for 5 minutes before serving.

Venison loin with spiced braised pears and chestnut

SERVES 4

PEARS

2 tsp ground cinnamon

½ tsp ground cumin

1 nutmeg, freshly grated

½ tsp Chinese 5-spice powder

4 pears (Comice or
    Conference), peeled

125g unsalted butter

CHESTNUT PURÉE

100g cooked chestnuts, chopped

125ml semi-skimmed or whole milk

½ tsp table salt

1 tbsp chestnut liqueur (Crème
    de Chataigne – optional)

SPROUTS

15g unsalted butter

6 Brussels sprouts, halved
    lengthways

¼ tsp table salt

25ml chicken or vegetable stock

VENISON

4 portions venison loin
    (approximately 80g each)

1 tbsp vegetable oil

1 tsp table salt

25g unsalted butter

1 chestnut, freshly grated

1 For the pears, mix the spices together then coat the pears.

2 Place the butter in a deep braising tin and heat until foaming, then add the pears. Cook over a moderately high heat until the pears are golden on the outside and tender when a knife is inserted. Remove from the butter and allow to cool.

3 Chop each pear, cutting out the core, into eight slices.

4 For the chestnut purée, put all the ingredients into a saucepan, bring to a gentle simmer and continue simmering for 5 minutes. Blend until smooth and pass through a fine sieve.

5 For the sprouts, heat the butter in a small pan until foaming. Season the sprouts, add to the pan and cook until nicely browned. Add the stock and cook until the sprouts are tender.

6 To cook the venison, heat the vegetable oil in a frying pan over a moderate to high heat. Season the venison with the salt, then carefully add it to the hot oil and brown all over. Add the butter, allow to foam, then spoon it over the venison, turning regularly for a couple of minutes. Remove from the pan and allow to rest for 4 minutes.

7 When ready to serve, reheat the chestnut purée in a small saucepan, stirring regularly to ensure it does not catch. Reheat the pears and the sprouts in the oven or with a little butter in a frying pan. Carve the venison, cut the sprouts in half again and serve accompanied by the pears, chestnut purée and grated chestnut.

Scallops with pistachio, parsnip crème and crispy prosciutto

SERVES 4

PARSNIP CRÈME
15g unsalted butter
2 parsnips, peeled and diced
pinch curry powder
½ tsp table salt
150ml semi-skimmed
    or whole milk
1 tbsp clear honey
SCALLOPS
2 tbsp vegetable oil
4 large scallops, roe removed
¼ tsp curry powder
¼ tsp table salt

4 rashers prosciutto
25g pistachio nuts, grated

1 Place the butter in a medium-sized saucepan over a medium heat. When melted, add the parsnips, curry powder and salt. Cook gradually, colouring slightly, for 10 minutes. Add the milk and honey, and allow to simmer very gently until cooked through. Blend and pass through a fine sieve.

2 To cook the scallops, heat the oil in a heavy-based non-stick pan. When smoking, season the scallops with the curry powder and salt, then place them in the hot oil. Cook evenly all over, obtaining a nice golden colour.

3 Meanwhile, preheat the oven to 200°C/400°F/ gas mark 6 or the grill to high. Place the prosciutto on a baking tray and bake or grill until crispy. Slice finely.

4 To serve, place a spoonful of the hot parsnip purée on each plate and drag your spoon through. Slice each scallop into three and lay on each plate. Sprinkle with the pistachio crumb and prosciutto strips and serve immediately.

Roasted vegetable, spinach and mozzarella calzone

SERVES 6–8

DOUGH
250g strong bread flour
1 tbsp fast-action dried yeast
1 tsp caster or granulated sugar
125ml water
50ml extra-virgin olive oil,
    plus extra for greasing
½ tsp table salt

FILLING
1 sweet potato, peeled and sliced
    into 5mm-thick slices
½ butternut squash, peeled and
    sliced into 5mm-thick slices
2 tbsp vegetable oil
½ tsp table salt
1kg spinach
100g sundried tomatoes
100g tomato purée
1 × 290g packet baby mozzarella
    balls, quartered
100g flame-roasted red peppers
¼ bunch parsley, chopped
½ tsp coarsely ground black pepper
25ml semi-skimmed or whole milk

1 Mix together all the ingredients for the dough and knead for 5 minutes. Place in an oiled bowl, cover and leave somewhere warm to double in volume for 20–30 minutes.

2 Meanwhile, preheat the oven to 180°C/350°F/ gas mark 4. Place the sweet potato and squash in a roasting tin with the oil and salt, and bake for 15–20 minutes until golden.

3 Bring a large pan of salted water to the boil and blanch the spinach for 30 seconds, then place under running water until cool. Squeeze all the water out of the spinach with your hands, then chop roughly.

4 Mix the sundried tomatoes with the tomato purée and set aside.

5 When the dough is ready, turn it out on to a floured surface and knead for another 5 minutes. Divide it into two balls, then roll out each one to a disc 25cm in diameter.

6 Place one circle of dough on an oiled baking tray. Layer the roasted sweet potato and squash, spinach, mozzarella, red peppers, tomato mixture and parsley on the dough circle. Sprinkle the black pepper over the top, then brush the edges of the dough with water. Place the other circle of dough on top and press the edges together to seal. Brush with milk, then bake for 15–20 minutes or until golden and cooked through.

Roast beef and potato-filled yorkies

SERVES 8

YORKSHIRE PUDDINGS
150g plain flour
150ml semi-skimmed
    or whole milk
3 medium free-range eggs
½ tsp table salt
8 tsp vegetable oil

FILLING
2 tbsp vegetable oil
2 medium onions, peeled
    and sliced
¼ bunch flat-leaf parsley,
    leaves chopped
¼ bunch tarragon,
    leaves chopped
8 large (or 12 medium)
    leftover roast potatoes,
    sliced thinly
12 slices leftover roast beef
2 tsp horseradish
8 tsp crème fraîche

1 Preheat the oven to 200°C/400°F/gas mark 6.

2 Blend the flour, milk, eggs and salt together until smooth.

3 Put the 8 tsp vegetable oil in eight large muffin tins and place in the oven for 5 minutes, positioning them where you can pour the batter in easily (ensure a baking tray is directly underneath to catch the splatter).

4 When the oil begins to smoke, pour the batter in and bake for 10–15 minutes until the puddings are golden and cooked through. Remove from the oven and allow to cool slightly.

5 Heat the 2 tbsp vegetable oil a large frying pan and fry the onions until caramelized. Add the herbs and season well, then set aside.

6 Layer the potatoes, beef and onions inside the puddings and place back in the oven for 5 minutes to heat through. Mix the horseradish and crème fraîche together. Remove the puddings from the oven and serve with a large dollop of the horseradish cream.

Roasted quail with butternut squash and black olives

SERVES 4

SQUASH PURÉE
1 butternut squash, peeled
    and deseeded
50g unsalted butter
½ tsp table salt
½ tsp coarsely ground black pepper
100ml chicken stock

SQUASH SALAD
2 tbsp vegetable oil
4 sprigs thyme
½ tsp table salt
25g unsalted butter
50g pitted black olives, chopped
50g cashew nuts, toasted
    and roughly chopped
2 tbsp pumpkin seed oil (optional)

QUAIL
500ml chicken stock
2 sprigs thyme
2 sprigs rosemary
½ bulb garlic, halved lengthways
4 quail
2 tbsp vegetable oil
pinch table salt
pinch coarsely ground pepper
2 knobs unsalted butter
coriander cress to garnish
    (or small coriander leaves)

1 Dice the top part of the squash into neat 1cm cubes, reserving the trim. Then dice the bottom part and keep separate.

2 Place the butter in a saucepan over a moderate heat and allow to melt. Add the trim from the top of the squash, plus the diced bottom part, to the pan with the salt and pepper. Stir regularly until the liquid seeps from the squash then evaporates.

3 Add the stock and simmer gently until the squash is tender. Blitz together then pass through a fine sieve.

4 For the squash salad, place a frying pan on a moderate heat. Add the oil and, when hot, add the diced top part of the squash, thyme and seasoning. Keep moving until the dice begin to brown, then add the butter and roast until golden.

5 For the quail, bring the stock to the boil with the herbs and garlic, then remove from the heat. Add the quail and remove after 3 minutes.

6 Heat the vegetable oil in a large frying pan over a moderate to high heat. Season the quail, then add them to the hot pan and brown all over. Add the butter and baste the birds until they are golden. Remove and set aside to rest for 5 minutes.

7 To serve, remove the breasts from the quail as you would from a chicken. Place them under a hot grill, skin side up, for a couple of minutes to warm them through.

8 Spoon a quarter of the squash purée on to each plate and swoosh it up the plate. Mix the squash dice with the olives, cashew nuts and, if using, pumpkin seed oil, add to the plate, then place the quail breasts on top. Garnish with a little cress and serve.

Monkfish with chorizo crust and spiced beans

SERVES 4

CHORIZO CRUST

100g chorizo, skin removed
   and sliced thinly
1 tsp unsalted butter
100g wholegrain bread,
   crusts removed
½ tsp smoked paprika
1 clove garlic, peeled and crushed
2 tbsp blanched almonds, toasted
   and finely chopped
pinch table salt

MONKFISH

4 pieces monkfish tail
   (approximately 100g each)
2 tbsp vegetable oil
1 tbsp unsalted butter

SPICED BEANS

150g white beans, soaked overnight
   and drained
1 carrot, peeled
2 onions, peeled, 1 halved and 1 sliced
1 stick celery
¼ bunch thyme
200ml chicken or vegetable stock
2 tbsp vegetable oil
2 cloves garlic, peeled and crushed
3 tbsp tomato purée
1 tsp turmeric
1 tsp smoked paprika
1 tsp ground cumin
300g ripe cherry tomatoes
½ tsp table salt
½ tsp coarsely ground black pepper
¼ bunch flat-leaf parsley, chopped

1 Place all the ingredients for the chorizo crust into a food processor and whiz until a paste has formed.

2 On a piece of clingfilm, spread one quarter of the crust mix into the length and circumference of a piece of monkfish. Fold the clingfilm over the fish and roll until it forms a sausage. Tie the ends to tighten the clingfilm, then place in the fridge. Repeat with the remaining three pieces of monkfish.

3 Place the drained beans into a saucepan with the carrot, halved onion, celery and thyme. Add the chicken or vegetable stock. Top up with cold water to cover and bring to a gentle simmer. Cook for 15–20 minutes until the beans are soft, then strain, reserving the liquid.

4 Heat 1 tbsp of the vegetable oil in a medium-sized frying pan over a moderate to high heat. Add the sliced onion and the garlic and cook until soft. Add the tomato purée, turmeric, paprika and cumin.

5 In another frying pan, heat the remaining oil until smoking, toss in the cherry tomatoes and seasoning and brown. Add the beans to the tomato-purée mixture with the reserved cooking stock. Allow to simmer gently. Add the cherry tomatoes and adjust the seasoning if necessary.

6 To cook the monkfish, heat the vegetable oil in a non-stick frying pan over a moderate heat. Carefully unwrap the monkfish from the clingfilm and place in the pan. Brown lightly all over, then add the butter and continue cooking for around 5 minutes, until the fish is cooked through. Add the chopped parsley to the beans and serve with the monkfish.

Herbed garlic bread with bacon and pine nut crumble

SERVES 4

BREAD

250g strong bread flour,
plus extra for dusting
1 tsp fast-action dried yeast
125ml tepid water
50ml olive oil, plus extra
for greasing
1 tsp caster or granulated sugar
1 tsp table salt
4 cloves garlic, peeled and crushed
¼ bunch flat-leaf parsley,
leaves chopped
¼ bunch thyme leaves

CRUMBLE

4 rashers unsmoked back bacon
50g pine nuts
50ml extra-virgin olive oil
1 tsp Maldon sea salt flakes
coarsely ground black pepper

1 Mix together all the bread ingredients, except the parsley and thyme. Knead for 5 minutes, then place in an oiled bowl, cover and leave in a warm place to double in volume.

2 While the bread is proving, make the crumble. Preheat the oven to 180°C/350°F/gas mark 4. Lay the bacon on a baking tray and bake for 10–15 minutes until crispy.

3 Put the pine nuts on another baking tray and bake for 5–10 minutes until golden. Roughly chop the bacon and pine nuts together and set aside.

4 When the dough has proved, place it on a lightly floured surface and knead in the herbs. Shape into a flat loaf and place on an oiled baking tray.

5 Press your fingers into the top of the bread to make small indentations and sprinkle with the pine nut and bacon crumble.

6 Drizzle the olive oil over the top, then the sea salt and pepper. Cover the bread and allow it to rise until doubled in volume again (this will take 20–30 minutes). Turn up the oven to 200°C/400°F/gas mark 6 and bake for 15–20 minutes until lightly golden. This bread is delicious with any soup.

1 Heat the oil in a deep fryer or a large saucepan.

2 Mix the spices, flours, salt and water together until a smooth batter is formed, adding more water if the mixture is too thick. Drop a small amount of the batter into the oil to check it is ready: if it bubbles and rises to the surface, then you can begin.

3 Coat the courgette batons in the batter, removing any excess batter, then drop them individually into the hot oil.

4 When lightly golden, remove with a slotted spoon on to a paper towel. Serve immediately.

55

Crispy courgette frites

SERVES 4

vegetable oil for deep frying
½ tsp ground cumin
½ tsp curry powder
2 tbsp cornflour
2 tbsp plain flour
½ tsp table salt
100ml sparkling water or soda water
4 courgettes, sliced into thin batons
     (approximately 8cm × 1cm × 1cm)

Seared scallops with black bean and ham hock

SERVES 4

1 ham hock (approximately 500g)

COOKING LIQUID
1 carrot, peeled and halved
1 stalk celery
1 onion, peeled and halved
½ bulb garlic
1 bay leaf
½ bunch thyme
8 white peppercorns
3 star anise
1 × 75g tin salted black beans,
    20g of them roughly chopped

SCALLOPS
1 tbsp vegetable oil
4 large scallops, roe removed
½ tsp curry powder mixed
    with 1 tsp table salt

1 Place the ham hock under cold running water for 20 minutes, then put it in a large saucepan with all the cooking-liquid ingredients except for the chopped black beans. Top up with enough water to cover, bring to the boil, then simmer very gently for 1–2 hours or until the meat separates easily from the bone. Remove the ham hock and allow to cool slightly, then pick the meat from the bone in large pieces.

2 Strain the stock into a clean saucepan, add the chopped black beans and bring to the boil. Simmer until reduced by half, skimming the fat and foam off the top regularly.

3 Heat the vegetable oil in a heavy-based non-stick frying pan. Dust each side of the scallops with the curry powder and salt. When the oil is smoking, carefully place the scallops in the pan. Cook evenly on each side for 3–5 minutes, depending on their size. Allow to rest for a couple of minutes, then slice.

4 Slice the ham hock, add to the black bean broth and heat through. Serve with the sliced scallops on top.

Cod, leek and blue cheese pies

MAKES 4

COD

400ml semi-skimmed
    or whole milk
100ml fish or chicken stock
¼ bunch thyme
½ bulb garlic, peeled and
    halved crossways
1 bay leaf
500g cod

100g unsalted butter
½ tsp table salt
2 leeks, white part only, sliced
100ml chicken stock
50g plain flour
125g your favourite blue
    cheese, crumbled
½ bunch flat-leaf parsley,
    leaves chopped
1 medium free-range egg yolk
4 puff-pastry discs, 3mm thick,
    to overlap the rim of each
    pie dish by 1cm

1 Place the milk, stock, thyme, garlic and bay leaf in a deep non-stick frying pan and warm gently; do not boil.

2 Season the cod, then add it to the liquid and allow to poach gently for 5–8 minutes, until it is just cooked through and flakes easily. Remove the fish and lay on paper towels. Strain the poaching liquid through a fine sieve and reserve.

3 Put 50g of the butter in a deep frying pan over a moderate to high heat. Add the leeks, season well and cook for 3–4 minutes until lightly coloured. Add the chicken stock and cook the leeks for a further 5 minutes until almost cooked through, then set aside.

4 Melt the remaining butter in a medium-sized saucepan over a moderate heat. Whisk in the flour and cook for a couple of minutes. Add a little of the fish-poaching liquid and whisk well. Add the remaining liquid and continue to stir until the mixture has thickened and has lost the raw flour taste.

5 Divide the cod, leeks and blue cheese evenly between four individual pie dishes. Add the parsley to the white sauce, adjust the seasoning if necessary, then spoon into the pie dishes.

6 Brush the top of the inside of each dish with a little egg yolk, then lay the pastry over the top, sealing it at the top edge and over the dish. Slice the excess pastry off. At this stage either put the pies in the fridge to bake later, or preheat the oven to 180°C/350°F/gas mark 4.

7 Before baking, brush the pastry lids with egg yolk and make two slits for the steam to escape. Bake for 20–25 minutes until the pastry is golden. Allow to rest for a couple of minutes before serving.

Beef fillet with braised baby carrots and parsnip gratin

SERVES 6

PARSNIP GRATIN
100ml white wine
½ bunch thyme leaves
2 bay leaves
150ml single or double cream
350ml semi-skimmed or whole milk
1 tbsp clear honey
2 nutmegs, freshly grated
½ tsp table salt
4 large parsnips (or 6 small), peeled
BEEF SAUCE
2 tbsp vegetable oil
80g beef trim or rump steak, diced
1 onion, peeled and diced
1 carrot, peeled and diced
1 stalk celery, diced
2 cloves garlic
1 tbsp tomato purée
4 whole black peppercorns
200ml red wine
300ml beef or chicken stock
½ tsp table salt
½ tsp Bovril or Marmite
1 bay leaf
½ bunch tarragon
BRAISED CARROTS
1 tbsp vegetable oil
12 baby carrots
salt and coarsely ground black pepper
25g unsalted butter
¼ bunch thyme leaves
2 cloves garlic
50ml chicken or vegetable stock
BEEF
2 tbsp vegetable oil
400–500g piece of beef fillet
1 tsp table salt
25g unsalted butter

1 Preheat the oven to 180°C/350°F/gas mark 4.

2 For the parsnip gratin, place the wine, thyme and bay leaves into a medium-sized saucepan over a moderate heat. Bring to the boil then simmer to reduce by two thirds. Add the cream, milk, honey, nutmeg and salt, then simmer very gently until the liquid has further reduced by a quarter.

3 Slice the parsnips thinly, lengthways, into strips. Layer with the wine and cream mixture in a small loaf tin or terrine mould, pressing the parsnips down as much as possible. Place in a roasting tin and bake for 25–30 minutes until brown on top and a knife goes easily through the centre. Slice into portions when cool.

4 For the beef sauce, heat 1 tbsp of the vegetable oil in a saucepan over a high heat. Season the beef trim or steak and fry until dark golden. Remove and set aside.

5 Add the onion, carrot, celery and garlic to the pan with the remaining oil and brown. Add the tomato purée, peppercorns and red wine. Simmer gently until you have a syrup-like consistency, then add the remaining ingredients. Simmer for 30 minutes, skimming regularly to remove any fat. Strain and check the seasoning.

6 For the carrots, heat the oil in a frying pan. Add the carrots and seasoning and brown well. Add the butter, thyme and garlic, and cook for 2 minutes. Add the stock and cook until tender.

7 To cook the beef fillet, heat the vegetable oil in a large ovenproof frying pan over a moderate heat. Season the beef, then lay it carefully in the pan and brown it all over. Add the butter and, when foaming, spoon it over the beef, and turn the meat a few times to coat thoroughly.

8 Place the entire frying pan in the hot oven for 5 minutes. Remove it, turn the beef over, then cook for a further 3 minutes. Remove the beef from the pan and allow it to rest for 5 minutes.

9 To serve, reheat the parsnip gratin in the oven at 200°C/400°F/gas mark 6 for 8 minutes, then spoon it on to warm plates. Add the carrots and beef, and finish with the sauce.

MARCUS WAREING GRILL ROOM

Aromatic sticky sweet chicken legs

SERVES 4

MARINADE
4 tbsp clear honey
6 tbsp soy sauce
3 tbsp hoisin sauce
3 cloves garlic, peeled
    and crushed
75g fresh root ginger, peeled
    and finely diced
2 star anise, dry-fried and ground
½ medium-sized red chilli,
    finely diced
1 stalk lemongrass,
    finely diced

8 chicken drumsticks or thighs

1 Mix the ingredients for the marinade together, smother over the chicken pieces and allow to marinate in the fridge for at least 6 hours, or overnight if possible.

2 Preheat the oven to 200°C/400°F/gas mark 6. Place the chicken in a roasting tin lined with tinfoil and bake in the oven, turning regularly, for 25–35 minutes, or until the juices run clear.

Beef and black bean hash with fried eggs and chips

SERVES 4

HASH
3 tbsp vegetable oil
600g braising steak
1 onion, peeled and quartered
½ bulb garlic, peeled and halved
    lengthways
2 sticks celery, quartered
1 carrot, peeled and quartered
50g salted black beans, half of
    them roughly chopped
1 tbsp tomato purée
500ml beef stock
4 tbsp soy sauce
1 tbsp Worcestershire sauce
1 tsp sesame oil
½ tsp coarsely ground black pepper

CHIPS
6 large potatoes (Maris Piper or
    King Edward), peeled and cut
    into chips
vegetable oil for deep frying

EGGS
4 medium free-range eggs
1 tbsp vegetable oil

1 For the hash, place 1 tbsp of the vegetable oil in a saucepan. When hot, season the beef and fry until browned. Remove and set aside.

2 Add another tablespoon of oil and fry the onion, garlic, celery, carrot and the whole black beans until browned. Add the tomato purée, then the stock, soy sauce and Worcestershire sauce.

3 Add the browned beef, cover the pan and simmer very gently for 1½ hours or until the beef is tender.

4 Remove the beef, strain the liquid and put it back on the heat to reduce to one quarter. Meanwhile, break up the beef and mix with the chopped black beans, the sesame oil and the pepper. Add the reduced liquid and mix well.

5 For the chips, place the potato sticks in seasoned cold water and simmer very gently for 7 minutes or until just tender. Strain and allow to cool.

6 Heat the vegetable oil in a deep-fat fryer or large pan to around 160°C or until an uncooked chip bubbles to the top. Fry the chips in batches and season well when you remove them from the hot oil.

7 For the hash, heat the remaining tablespoon of vegetable oil in a non-stick frying pan and fry the beef until hot. Set aside, then fry the eggs over a moderate heat until cooked to your liking. Serve the hash and eggs with the chips.

Five-spiced honey pork chops

SERVES 4

1 cinnamon stick
1 tsp fennel seeds
1 star anise
½ tsp coarsely ground black pepper
½ tsp whole cloves
6 tbsp clear honey
½ tsp table salt
8 pork chops (100–120g each)
1 tbsp vegetable oil

1 Dry-fry all the spices, then grind them together, using either a spice grinder or a pestle and mortar, and pass through a sieve to remove any large pieces.

2 Mix the ground spices with the honey and salt, then rub the mixture over the pork chops. Cover and refrigerate for 2 hours.

3 Preheat the oven to 180°C/350°F/gas mark 4.

4 Heat the vegetable oil in a large frying pan over a moderate to high heat, then brown the chops on both sides.

5 Place the chops in a foil-lined roasting dish and bake for a further 10–15 minutes until the juices run clear. Allow to rest for 5 minutes, then serve.

Spiced sweet potato wedges with chilli sour cream

SERVES 4

WEDGES
1 tsp ground cumin
1 tsp ground coriander
½ tsp ground cinnamon
1 tsp Chinese 5-spice powder
½ tsp table salt
1 tsp caster or granulated sugar
4 large sweet potatoes, peeled
   and cut into wedges
100ml vegetable oil

CHILLI SOUR CREAM
250g sour cream
1 medium green chilli, seeds
   removed, then finely diced
½ onion, peeled and finely chopped
½ bunch coriander, chopped
½ tsp table salt
1 tsp sweet chilli sauce

1 Preheat the oven to 200°C/400°F/gas mark 6.

2 Place all the spices in a plastic bag with the salt and sugar. Add the sweet potato wedges and shake the bag to coat the wedges evenly. Put the oil in a large roasting tin and add the wedges. Bake for 30–40 minutes, turning the wedges regularly.

3 For the chilli sour cream, mix all the ingredients together. Adjust the seasoning if necessary.

1 Preheat the oven to 180°C/350°F/gas mark 4.

2 Lightly grease six large muffin tins. Divide the pastry into six even-sized pieces and line the tins, leaving the excess pastry hanging over the edges.

3 Very lightly beat the eggs, then add the remaining ingredients. Divide the mixture between the six lined tins and place them in the oven for 10–15 minutes or until the eggs are only slightly wobbly in the centre.

68

Bacon and egg pies

MAKES 6

1 sheet pre-rolled puff pastry
6 medium free-range eggs
6 rashers shoulder or back bacon,
    rind removed, diced
¼ bunch tarragon, leaves chopped
60g Emmental cheese, grated
½ tsp table salt
coarsely ground black pepper

Barbecued sweetcorn with smoky butter

SERVES 4

SMOKY BUTTER
50g unsalted butter, softened
½ tsp smoked paprika
½ tsp table salt
½ medium-sized red chilli,
    finely diced
½ clove garlic, peeled
    and crushed
¼ bunch coriander, chopped
SWEETCORN
4 cobs sweetcorn, husks
    removed
1 tbsp vegetable oil

1 Mix all the ingredients for the butter together. Form the mixture into a sausage shape, wrap it in clingfilm and place it in the fridge for 30 minutes.

2 Allow the barbecue to heat up. When hot, rub the corn cobs with the vegetable oil then place them on the barbecue until they are cooked through and have turned a deep colour on the outside.

3 Dice the butter and dot it over the top of each cob. Serve immediately.

Pork and pickle pies

MAKES 6

PASTRY

150g plain white flour, plus
    extra for dusting
100g wholemeal flour
½ tsp table salt
150g unsalted butter, cold
    and diced
1 medium free-range egg
1 tbsp cold water

FILLING

100g lean back bacon
400g pork shoulder, boned
    and chopped
200g pork sausagemeat
2 medium onions, peeled and
    finely chopped
½ bunch sage, leaves chopped
½ bunch thyme leaves
¼ bunch flat-leaf parsley,
    leaves chopped
1 clove garlic, peeled and
    crushed
½ nutmeg, freshly grated
½ tsp ground mace
½ tsp table salt
coarsely ground black pepper
240g Branston pickle

FOR GLAZING

1 medium free-range egg yolk

1 Lightly grease a large 6-hole muffin tray and set aside.

2 To make the pastry, mix the flours and salt together, then rub in the butter until the mixture resembles breadcrumbs. Add the egg and water and mix to a stiff dough.

3 Cover and leave to rest for 20 minutes in the fridge, then roll out on a floured surface to 5mm thick. Cut out six large circles (to fit inside the muffin moulds) and six smaller circles (for the lids). Line the moulds with the base circles and place the lids between squares of baking paper. Refrigerate until ready to use.

4 For the filling, put the bacon and two thirds of the pork shoulder into a food processor and pulse into small chunks (do not mince). Remove from the bowl and mix with the rest of the pork shoulder and the remaining ingredients, except for half of the pickle.

5 Preheat the oven to 165°C/325°F/gas mark 3. Half fill the pastry cases with the pork mix, then add a spoonful of the remaining pickle and top up with more pork mix.

6 Brush the edges of each pastry lid with a little water and press tightly on the pie cases to seal. Crimp the edges of the pastry with a fork and trim to leave only a 1cm edge. Brush the lids with egg yolk, then slash a hole in the top of the pastry. Bake for 30 minutes, then allow to cool in the tins before removing.

Lamb and roast garlic pots with rosemary dumplings

MAKES 4

GARLIC

3 bulbs garlic, halved lengthways,
    skins still on
1 tbsp vegetable oil
½ tsp table salt

HOTPOT

2 tbsp vegetable oil
400g braising lamb, diced
2 tbsp plain flour
1 tsp table salt
1 medium onion, peeled and diced
1 tbsp tomato purée
1 tsp cumin seeds, toasted and
    lightly crushed
250ml red wine
2 litres chicken or vegetable stock
2 bay leaves
½ bunch rosemary
½ bunch thyme
½ tsp coarsely ground black pepper
1 carrot, peeled and diced
1 parsnip, peeled and diced
1 sweet potato, peeled and diced

DUMPLINGS

175g plain flour
2 tsp baking powder
½ tsp table salt
¼ bunch rosemary, leaves finely chopped
100g unsalted butter, diced and cold
125ml semi-skimmed or whole milk

1 Preheat the oven to 180°C/350°F/gas mark 4. Place the garlic halves in tinfoil and drizzle with the oil, sprinkle with the salt and then gather up the foil to seal lightly. Place in the oven for 25 minutes.

2 For the hotpot, heat the oil in a large saucepan over a moderate heat. Coat the lamb in the flour and salt and brown well. Remove from the pan and place in a colander.

3 Add the onions, tomato purée and cumin to the pan and lightly caramelize. Add the red wine and reduce to a syrup. Add the stock, lamb, herbs and pepper to the pan and allow to simmer gently, covered, for 45 minutes.

4 Squeeze the cloves of roasted garlic from their skins and add to the pan along with the remaining vegetables. Simmer gently for a further 30 minutes.

5 For the dumplings, combine the flour, baking powder, salt and rosemary, then rub in the butter. Add enough milk to mix to a firm dough. Roll the dough into sixteen small balls and refrigerate until the lamb is cooked.

6 Divide the lamb into four deep ramekins or pots, add four dumplings to each, then cover with lids or tinfoil. Bake in the oven for 15 minutes, then allow to rest for 5 minutes before serving.

Home-made beef burgers with caramelized onions and emmental cheese

MAKES 4

BURGERS
500g beef mince
1 medium onion, peeled and diced
2 cloves garlic, peeled and crushed
1 medium free-range egg,
    lightly beaten
50g fresh brown breadcrumbs
¼ bunch flat-leaf parsley, leaves
    chopped
¼ bunch tarragon, leaves chopped
1 tbsp tomato purée
2 tbsp soy sauce
2 tbsp tomato ketchup
½ tsp coarsely ground black pepper
½ tsp table salt

CARAMELIZED ONIONS
25g unsalted butter
3 medium onions, peeled and sliced
¼ bunch thyme leaves
½ tsp table salt

1 tbsp vegetable oil
4 slices Emmental cheese
1 loaf ciabatta, halved lengthways
2 tbsp extra-virgin olive oil
4 tbsp hummus
4 small handfuls rocket

1 Mix the ingredients for the burgers together. Fry a little of the mixture to check the seasoning; adjust if necessary. Shape into four patties and refrigerate.

2 For the caramelized onions, melt the butter in a medium-sized frying pan, add the sliced onions, thyme and salt, and cook for around 20–25 minutes until golden and sticky.

3 Heat the vegetable oil in a large frying pan and brown the burgers until cooked through. Remove them from the heat and place a slice of cheese on top of each to melt gently.

4 Brush the inside of the ciabatta loaf with the olive oil and grill or toast lightly. Spread the top half with hummus, then lay the beef patties on the other half. Add the onions and rocket and sandwich the two halves together. Cut into four and serve while hot.

Fillet of salmon with baby leeks, lobster, crème fraîche and tarragon

SERVES 4

150g crème fraîche
1½ tsp table salt
1 tsp capers, finely chopped
¼ bunch tarragon leaves,
    finely chopped
25g unsalted butter
4 tbsp chicken stock
16 baby leeks, blanched
    and refreshed
100g lobster meat, from
    the claw
2 tbsp vegetable oil
4 portions salmon fillet,
    pin-boned, skin on and
    scored using a sharp knife

1 First whisk the crème fraîche, then add a ½ tsp of the salt, the capers and half the chopped tarragon.

2 Heat the butter and chicken stock together with another ½ tsp of the salt and whisk until combined. Remove 2 tbsp of this liquid and set aside, then add the leeks to the mixture in the pan to warm through.

3 Place the lobster meat in a small saucepan with the reserved liquid and gently heat through.

4 Heat the vegetable oil in a large non-stick frying pan. Season the salmon on both sides with the remaining ½ tsp of salt. When the oil is hot, add the fish to the pan, skin side down. Shake the pan gently to allow the oil to get under the skin so that it browns evenly. Leave for 4 minutes, then remove the pan from the heat and gently turn the fillets over using a spatula.

5 Add the remaining chopped tarragon to the warmed lobster, then place four leeks in the centre of each of four plates. Arrange the lobster meat around the plates, then lay the salmon skin side up on top of the leeks. Place a spoonful of the crème fraîche mixture on to the salmon and serve immediately.

Roasted monkfish with braised shallot and olive-crusted potatoes

SERVES 2

BRAISED SHALLOT
15g unsalted butter
2 large banana shallots, peeled
    and halved lengthways
½ tsp table salt
1 tsp balsamic vinegar
50ml chicken or vegetable stock
1 sprig thyme

OLIVE-CRUSTED POTATOES
4 large new potatoes, scrubbed,
    boiled then chilled
50g pitted black olives, dried
    in a low-temperature oven
    for 2 hours, crumbled
1 tbsp olive oil

MONKFISH
50g unsalted butter
2 portions monkfish tail
    (approximately 150g each)
½ tsp table salt
¼ tsp curry powder

deep-fried chilli, sprigs of
    coriander and mint, and
    curry powder to garnish

1 For the shallots, heat the butter in a frying pan until it foams. Add the seasoned shallots, and allow to brown for around 5 minutes. Add the balsamic vinegar, then the stock and sprig of thyme. Allow to cook for a further 10 minutes until the shallots are cooked through.

2 For the potatoes, cut into batons then coat in the dried-olive crumble. Slice into squares and rub with a little olive oil, then set aside.

3 To cook the monkfish, heat the butter in a non-stick frying pan over a moderate to high heat and allow to foam. Dust the monkfish in the curry powder and salt, then roast in the foaming butter for 3–5 minutes. Allow to rest for a couple of minutes before serving.

4 To serve, separate the layers of the shallot and arrange on each plate. Slice the monkfish in half and arrange on top of the shallot. Place the potato squares around the side, then dust the plate with a little curry powder and garnish. Serve immediately.

Roasted beef sirloin with mushrooms, brandy and roasted potatoes

SERVES 6–8

SAUCE

1 tbsp vegetable oil
2 onions, peeled and sliced
½ tsp coarsely ground black pepper
250g button mushrooms, sliced
¼ bunch thyme (tied with string)
1 clove garlic, crushed
400ml brandy
200ml red wine
¼ bunch tarragon (tied with string)
250ml chicken stock
200g crème fraîche
¼ bunch tarragon, leaves chopped
½ tsp table salt

BEEF

2 tbsp vegetable oil
beef sirloin (approximately 2kg)
1 tsp table salt
½ tsp coarsely ground black pepper
50g unsalted butter
1 bulb garlic, halved lengthways
¼ bunch thyme
¼ bunch rosemary

ROASTED POTATOES

500g small roasting potatoes,
    halved
4 tbsp vegetable oil
1 tsp Maldon sea salt
½ tsp paprika
½ bunch thyme

1 For the sauce, heat the vegetable oil in a large saucepan over a moderate to high heat. Add the onions, pepper, mushrooms, thyme and garlic, then cook until soft and lightly browned. Add the brandy, red wine and the tied bunch of tarragon and reduce to a syrup. Add the chicken stock and simmer gently to reduce by half. Remove the thyme and tarragon, mix in the crème fraîche and the chopped tarragon leaves. Taste and adjust the seasoning if necessary.

2 For the beef, preheat the oven to 220°C/ 425°F/gas mark 7. Heat the vegetable oil in an ovenproof frying pan big enough to fit the sirloin. Season the sirloin all over and, when the oil is very hot, gently brown all over. Add the butter, garlic and herbs and allow the butter to foam. Spoon it over the meat to baste, turning often, for 5 minutes. Put the entire frying pan into the oven and turn the sirloin over every 5 minutes, basting with the butter. Remove after 15 minutes for rare, 22 minutes for medium and 30 minutes for well done. Allow to rest for 10 minutes before carving.

3 For the potatoes, put all the ingredients into a roasting tin, making sure the potatoes are well coated in oil, and roast in the oven with the beef until golden.

Rack of lamb with butternut squash terrine and mustard cabbage

SERVES 4

TERRINE

100g unsalted butter
½ bunch rosemary, leaves chopped
1 butternut squash, top part only,
  peeled and thinly sliced
1 tsp table salt

LAMB

2 tbsp vegetable oil
½ tsp table salt
4 portions lamb rack
  (approximately 150g each)
2 tbsp butter

MUSTARD CABBAGE

½ Savoy cabbage, very thinly sliced
1 tbsp Pommery or wholegrain
  mustard
2 tbsp crème fraîche
½ tsp table salt

Maldon sea salt, thyme leaves
  and olive oil to garnish

1 Preheat the oven to 180°C/350°F/gas mark 4. Place the butter and rosemary in a small saucepan and bring to a gentle simmer. Allow the butter to turn a slightly golden colour and the rosemary to infuse for 10 minutes. Pass carefully through a fine sieve as it will be very hot.

2 Layer the squash in a baking dish approximately 15cm × 10cm, placing a spoonful of the melted butter and a small sprinkle of salt between each layer.

3 Bake in the oven for 30 minutes, pressing down on the squash at least 4 times throughout cooking, then remove and chill in the fridge immediately. When completely cool, cut into small cubes.

4 For the lamb, heat the vegetable oil in a heavy-based ovenproof frying pan until smoking. Season the lamb, add to the pan and brown all over. Add the butter and allow to foam, spooning it over the top of the racks. Place the frying pan in the oven for 5–10 minutes depending on how well you like your lamb cooked. Remove and allow to rest for 5 minutes before carving.

5 Blanch the cabbage in boiling, salted water for 1 minute. Drain and cool quickly under running water, then squeeze out all of the excess moisture. Transfer to a small saucepan, add the mustard, crème fraîche and salt, and heat through.

6 When ready to serve, return the squash squares to the oven on a tray lined with baking paper for 10 minutes. Garnish with a little picked thyme and Maldon salt if you wish.

ORIENT

Chillies, lemongrass, coriander, ginger, fish sauce and limes all possess heady scents and crisp flavours that are unique and exotic. Although not everyone's initial choice, they add something special to any meal and, once tried, they are often loved.

For the recipes in this chapter I have taken my favourite oriental ingredients and dishes, and have adapted them to a more British style of cookery. I urge you to try, in particular, the Aromatic Braised and Roasted Whole Duck with Pancakes and Garnish (page 99), as it is a delicious and simple 'at home' take on Chinese crispy duck. Chicken and Avocado Rice Paper Rolls (page 92) is another refreshing recipe: try it on a summer's evening with friends, gathering round to make your own rolls for a really sociable occasion. For a unique and light canapé, try the Cucumber, Pickled Ginger, Sesame and Tuna Sushi (page 90).

Fragrant asian hot pot with prawns

SERVES 4

20 raw, unpeeled tiger prawns
　　(with heads on)

STOCK
2 tbsp vegetable oil
2 tbsp tom yum paste
1 tbsp tomato purée
1 stalk lemongrass, chopped
1 bunch coriander, leaves chopped,
　　stalks retained
100g fresh root ginger, peeled
　　and chopped
2 kaffir lime leaves (if available)
1 tbsp fish sauce
2 tbsp soft brown sugar
juice of 1 lime
3 star anise
½ tsp table salt
2 litres chicken or vegetable
　　stock, or water

1 tbsp vegetable oil
1 × 225g tin water chestnuts,
　　drained and sliced
1 × 225g tin bamboo shoots,
　　drained and sliced
200g mung bean sprouts
1 carrot, peeled and julienned
100g mangetout, halved
100g baby corn, sliced

1 Twist the heads off the prawns and peel off their shells, but do not discard. Make a small incision at the top of the meaty part of each prawn going all the way down to the tail, then remove the small pipe and discard. Cover the prawns and refrigerate.

2 For the stock, heat the vegetable oil in a large saucepan over a moderate to high heat. Add all the stock ingredients, including the coriander stalks but not the chopped leaves, and stir until lightly browned.

3 Add the prawn heads and shells and cook until most of the liquid has evaporated. Add the stock or water, bring to a gentle simmer and continue simmering for 30 minutes. Strain through a fine sieve into a clean saucepan and place back over a low heat.

4 Heat the 1 tbsp of vegetable oil in a non-stick frying pan until smoking. Season the prawns, then sear quickly, browning well.

5 Put the prawns into the broth, then bring to a simmer again and add the remaining ingredients. Serve immediately, garnishing with the chopped coriander leaves.

Chinese spiced pork buns

MAKES 12

PORK
1 tbsp vegetable oil
1 small pork shoulder
1 medium onion, peeled and diced
3 star anise, roughly chopped
1 cinnamon stick
1 tsp fennel seeds
½ tsp whole cloves
2 cloves garlic, peeled and crushed
½ tsp table salt
½ tsp coarsely ground black pepper
2 tbsp tomato purée
2 tbsp hoisin sauce
250ml Chinese cooking wine
     (Shaoxing)
1 litre beef, chicken or vegetable
     stock
DOUGH
125g plain flour
1 tbsp caster sugar
100ml warm water
½ tsp fast-action dried yeast
½ tsp baking powder
1 tbsp sesame oil, plus extra
     for greasing
¼ tsp table salt
FILLING
¼ bunch coriander
3 spring onions, finely sliced
60g water chestnuts, finely sliced

1 For the pork, heat the vegetable oil in a large saucepan over a medium to high heat. Season the shoulder then put it in the hot pan, skin side down, and brown all over. Remove it from the pan and set aside. Add the onion to the saucepan and brown.

2 Heat a frying pan and toast the spices until fragrant, then add them and the garlic to the onion in the saucepan and season. Cook for 2 minutes, then add the tomato purée, hoisin sauce and Chinese wine and allow to simmer for 5 minutes.

3 Return the pork to the pan and add the stock, then place a circle of baking paper on top. Allow to simmer very gently for 1 hour.

4 Meanwhile, mix all the ingredients for the dough together, but do not over-mix. Form into a ball, place in an oiled bowl, cover and set aside in a warm place for 30 minutes until doubled in volume.

5 Remove the pork from the stock and wrap it in tinfoil. Strain the cooking liquid into a clean saucepan and put it back over a moderate to high heat. Boil gently and reduce the liquid to a thick glaze. Shred the pork and mix it with the glaze.

6 Add the coriander, spring onions and water chestnuts. Adjust the seasoning if necessary. Roll the mixture into 12 balls (approximately 25g each) and place them in the fridge to firm up.

7 Divide the dough into 12 small balls, then roll into discs and place a spoonful of the pork mixture in the centre. Pinch the tops together and press well to seal. Place the buns on a square of baking paper, then place them in a steamer (bamboo or saucepan) over simmering water. Cook until they have puffed up and are no longer spongy. Serve immediately.

Cucumber, pickled ginger, sesame and tuna sushi

MAKES 20 PIECES

200g sashimi-grade yellowfin tuna
2 tbsp soy sauce
1 tbsp sesame oil
1 large cucumber
50g sesame seeds, toasted
50g pickled ginger
½ tsp Maldon sea salt

1 Cut the tuna into 20 small strips, each approximately 2.5cm long. Mix the soy sauce and sesame oil together and put in a bowl with the tuna. Allow to marinate for 20 minutes.

2 Peel the cucumber then, using a peeler, shave off ten long strips of flesh. Cut these in half across the middle, then lay them out on a board.

3 Shake the excess marinade off each strip of tuna, then roll them in the toasted sesame seeds. Place a piece of sesame-crusted tuna at one end of each piece of cucumber, add a piece of ginger, then roll up tightly.

4 To serve, stand each cucumber roll on its end and sprinkle with a little flaked sea salt.

Sticky lamb rice parcels

MAKES 12 PARCELS

MARINADE
4 tbsp oyster sauce
2 tbsp soy sauce
1 tsp tomato purée
½ medium-sized red chilli,
    deseeded and finely sliced
1 clove garlic, peeled and crushed
2 tbsp brown sugar

2 lamb neck fillets (approximately
    120g), cut into small dice
200g short-grain rice
½ tsp caster or granulated sugar
½ tsp table salt
2 star anise
2 cardamom pods
2 tbsp sesame oil
1 tbsp vegetable oil
¼ bunch coriander, chopped
12 lotus leaves or 12cm × 6cm
    rectangles baking paper

1 Mix all the ingredients for the marinade together and add the diced lamb. Cover and refrigerate overnight.

2 Put the rice in a saucepan with the sugar and salt. Cover with enough cold water to come 2cm above the rice. Place the star anise and cardamom pods on top, then cover with a lid and cook over a low to moderate heat for 15 minutes.

3 Remove the pan from the heat and allow to stand for a further 5 minutes. Remove the star anise and cardamom pods and stir in the sesame oil, then put the lid back on.

4 While the rice is cooking, heat the vegetable oil in a medium-sized frying pan, add the lamb and cook for 10 minutes until tender. Stir in the coriander, then leave to cool slightly.

5 To assemble the parcels, place a tablespoonful of rice in the centre of each lotus leaf or rectangle of baking paper. Flatten the rice, then add a spoonful of the lamb mixture in the centre. Put another spoonful of rice on top of the lamb mixture and flatten. Fold two opposite sides of the leaf or baking paper over the filling, then fold over the remaining two sides to form a parcel.

6 Bring a pan of water to a gentle simmer, put the parcels in a steamer over the water and steam for 10–15 minutes. Serve while hot.

Chicken and avocado rice paper rolls

MAKES 20

2 organic corn-fed chicken breasts
6 tbsp soy sauce
2 tbsp sweet chilli sauce
20 rice papers (12–15cm diameter)

DIPPING SAUCE
1 tsp vegetable oil
½ medium onion, peeled and
    finely diced
1 clove garlic, peeled and crushed
1 tbsp soy sauce
1 tbsp sweet chilli sauce
6 tbsp peanut butter
250ml water
pinch table salt

FILLING
50g roasted peanuts, chopped
½ iceberg lettuce, finely shredded
½ bunch mint, leaves chopped
½ bunch coriander leaves
50g pickled ginger
1 avocado, peeled, stoned
    and sliced

1 Preheat the oven to 165°C/325°F/gas mark 3. Smear the chicken in the soy and sweet chilli sauces, then wrap both breasts in tinfoil. Place on a baking tray and bake for 15 minutes, then remove from the oven and allow to rest for 10 minutes. Shred the meat with two forks when cool and leave it in the cooking juices.

2 For the dipping sauce, put the vegetable oil in a small saucepan over a low to moderate heat. Add the onion and garlic and cook until soft, then add the soy and chilli sauces and mix well. Stir in the peanut butter, then gradually add the water, mixing well after each addition. Remove from the heat and season with the pinch of salt, adjusting the amount if necessary.

3 To assemble the rolls, take a glass or earthenware dish, just larger than the rice papers, and pour in boiling water to a depth of 3–4cm. Add five rice papers and move them around, using a chopstick or spoon. Remove them after a couple of seconds, when they seem soft, and spread them carefully on a plate.

4 Fill each rice paper wrap by spooning a little shredded chicken and a portion of each of the filling ingredients into the centre; do not over-fill, or you will not be able to roll the wrap up. Fold two opposite edges of the rice paper into the centre, then fold the other edges over and place the rice paper roll seam side down on a serving plate. Repeat with the remaining rice papers, then serve with the dipping sauce.

Shredded chicken satay noodle soup

SERVES 4

2 tbsp vegetable oil
2 organic corn-fed chicken breasts
1 medium red chilli, finely sliced
1 medium onion, peeled and
    finely diced
2 cloves garlic, peeled and crushed
4 tbsp peanut butter
1 tbsp soy sauce
2 litres chicken or vegetable stock
1 × 400ml tin coconut milk
½ tsp table salt
100g thick rice noodles
50g peanuts, roasted and
    roughly chopped
½ bunch coriander, leaves
    chopped

1 Heat the vegetable oil in a large saucepan over a moderate heat. Quickly brown the chicken breasts all over, then remove and set aside.

2 Add the chilli, onion and garlic to the pan and brown. Stir in the peanut butter and soy sauce, then gradually mix in the stock.

3 Bring to a gentle simmer and add the chicken. Keep at a very low simmer for 30 minutes.

4 Using two forks, shred the chicken whilst in the soup. Add the coconut milk and the salt, adjusting the seasoning if necessary, and continue to simmer on the low heat.

5 Meanwhile, bring a large pan of salted water to the boil, add the rice noodles and cook until al dente. Drain, then add the noodles to the soup. Serve while hot, garnished with the peanuts and coriander.

Soft-shell crab with crispy mint, coriander and chilli

SERVES 2

vegetable oil for deep frying
½ bunch mint leaves
½ bunch coriander leaves, plus
    a few extra for garnishing
1 red chilli, sliced
½ tsp icing sugar
¼ tsp table salt

BATTER
1 tbsp plain flour
1 tbsp cornflour
½ tsp table salt
½ tsp caster sugar
¼ tsp chilli powder
¼ tsp curry powder
soda water to combine

2 soft-shell crabs

1 Take a saucepan large enough to accommodate the two crabs and half fill it with vegetable oil, then place over a moderate heat. When the temperature reaches 140°C put the mint, coriander and chilli carefully into the oil and remove after 2 minutes, using a sieve. Season immediately with the icing sugar and table salt and allow to drain on paper towels.

2 Increase the heat a little until the oil reaches 165°C, then whisk all the batter ingredients together with enough soda water to form a stiff batter. Coat the crabs in the batter, then carefully place them into the hot oil and allow them to brown. Remove and place on paper towels for a couple of minutes, then serve immediately with the crispy herbs and chilli.

Vegetable gyoza

MAKES 20

1 tbsp vegetable oil, plus a little
   extra for frying
80g fresh root ginger, peeled
   and finely diced
1 clove garlic, peeled and crushed
2 spring onions, finely sliced
¼ stalk lemongrass, finely chopped
½ tsp table salt
½ medium-sized green chilli,
   deseeded and finely chopped
¼ Savoy cabbage, finely shredded
½ × 225g tin water chestnuts,
   drained and finely diced
¼ bunch coriander, leaves chopped
1 tbsp sesame oil

DIPPING SAUCE
2 tbsp soy sauce
2 tbsp mirin
½ tsp wasabi paste
1 tsp sesame oil
½ tsp fish sauce

20 gyoza skins (if unavailable,
   use wonton wrappers)

1 Heat the 1 tbsp of vegetable oil in a medium-sized frying pan over a moderate heat. When hot, add the ginger, garlic, spring onions, lemongrass, salt and chilli, and cook until soft.

2 Add the cabbage and water chestnuts to the pan. Cook until the cabbage has broken down, then add the coriander and sesame oil. Set aside to cool.

3 For the dipping sauce, mix all the ingredients together and set aside.

4 Lay out five gyoza skins. Fill each with a teaspoonful of the vegetable mixture. Brush the edges of the skins with water, then fold them over diagonally and pinch the sides together to form a half-moon dumpling shape. Repeat with the remaining gyoza skins and mixture.

5 To serve, heat a medium-sized non-stick frying pan with a little vegetable oil and fry the parcels until golden. Serve while hot, accompanied by the dipping sauce.

Aromatic braised and roasted whole duck with pancakes and garnish

SERVES 4–6

1 small to medium duck (preferably
   Gressingham), giblets removed

MIREPOIX
1 onion, peeled and quartered
2 stalks celery, halved
1 leek, white only, halved
2 carrots, peeled and quartered
1 bulb garlic, halved lengthways
2 cinnamon sticks
3 star anise
1 orange, halved
2 red chillies, halved
¼ bunch coriander stalks
80g fresh root ginger, peeled
   and roughly chopped

250ml Madeira wine
2 litres chicken or vegetable stock
2 tbsp soy sauce
4 tbsp hoisin sauce
2 tbsp clear honey

PANCAKES
150g plain flour
¼ tsp table salt
125ml boiling water
2 tbsp sesame oil

GARNISH
1 bunch spring onions, finely
   julienned
1 cucumber, finely julienned
hoisin sauce

1 Heat a large saucepan over a moderate heat. When hot, add the duck and brown all over (strain some of the fat off during the browning). When golden all over, remove from the pan.

2 Put the *mirepoix* ingredients into the pan and brown well. Add the Madeira and simmer until it reaches a syrup-like consistency. Mix in the stock, soy and hoisin sauces, and the honey, then add the duck and cover with a lid. Simmer gently for 1½ hours.

3 To make the pancakes, put the flour and salt into a deep bowl. Pour in the boiling water. Mix well, then turn out on to a floured worktop and knead until silky (5–10 minutes). Cover with clingfilm and set aside for 20 minutes to rest.

4 Roll the dough into a sausage shape. Cut into 16 slices and keep covered with a damp cloth. Take one piece, dip one side in the sesame oil and flatten the dough with the palm of your hand. Roll it into a thin circle and lay it on a piece of baking paper. Repeat with the remaining slices and stack between baking paper. Heat a frying pan over a moderate heat and dry-fry the pancakes until cooked through. Stack between the paper again and cover with a damp cloth.

5 When it is cooked, carefully remove the duck from the stock using two slotted spoons and place it on a roasting tray lined with tinfoil. Cover with clingfilm. Preheat the oven to 200°C/400°F/gas mark 6.

6 Strain the cooking liquid into a clean saucepan and bring to the boil. Reduce the liquid by two thirds to form a gravy-like sauce. Brush the duck all over with the sauce, then heat through in the oven for 10 minutes until slightly crisp on the outside. Heat the pancakes in a steamer, then serve with the duck, spring onions, cucumber and hoisin sauce.

1 Place all the ingredients for the fish cakes, except for the fish itself, in a food processor and whiz until as smooth as possible. Add the fish and pulse until just combined. Shape into 12 patties and refrigerate until ready to cook.

2 For the dipping sauce, mix all the ingredients together and leave to infuse for a minimum of 30 minutes.

3 To cook the fish cakes, heat the oil in a large non-stick frying pan over a moderate to high heat. Cook the fish cakes on each side until nicely browned and cooked through. Serve while hot, accompanied by the dipping sauce.

Vietnamese fish cakes with hot and sour dipping sauce

SERVES 4

FISH CAKES
1 medium green chilli, finely chopped
2 stalks lemongrass, finely chopped
80g fresh root ginger, peeled and
    finely chopped
2 cloves garlic, peeled and crushed
1 bunch coriander, leaves chopped
1 tbsp fish sauce
1 tsp table salt
juice and zest of 1 lime
2 tbsp sesame oil
400–500g firm white fish fillets,
    such as hake or sole

DIPPING SAUCE
4 tbsp sweet chilli sauce
80g fresh root ginger, peeled and
    finely chopped
6 tbsp rice wine vinegar, or white
    wine vinegar
juice and zest of 1 lime
1 tsp palm sugar, finely chopped
    (or brown sugar)

2 tbsp vegetable oil

SPICE ROUTE

In the seventeenth century, a small island called Run, in the Banda archipelago, held the world's riches. They came from a tree called *Myristica fragrans* – to us, simply the nutmeg tree. Nutmeg was a spice held to have such powerful medicinal properties that men risked their lives to acquire it. Always costly, it rocketed in price after the doctors of Elizabethan London began claiming that their nutmeg pomanders were the only cure for the plague. In the Banda Islands, 10lb of nutmeg cost less than one English penny. In London, that same spice sold at a mark-up of a staggering 60,000 per cent. One small sackful was enough to set a man up for life, buying him a cottage in Holborn and a servant to attend to his needs.

Even in the East Indies, where spices grew like weeds, nutmeg was a rarity – a tree so fussy about climate and soil that it would grow only on the tiny cluster of Indonesian islands that formed the Banda archipelago, which were of such impossible remoteness that no one in Europe could be sure if they existed at all. In trying to sail there and back, many Englishmen lost their lives to scurvy and other deadly illnesses, pirate attacks and ferocious storms.

To me, spices are one of the most interesting ingredients in cooking. They can transform dishes from the somewhat ordinary to the sublime, especially through their aromas, which add tenfold to the anticipated flavour of a dish.

Blackened chilli belly of pork

SERVES 4-6

1 piece boned pork belly
    (1.5–2kg), rind scored
3 tbsp rock salt
3 medium red chillies,
    finely diced
200ml soy sauce
150g fresh root ginger,
    peeled and finely diced
4 tbsp demerara sugar
4 cloves garlic, peeled
    and crushed
3 tbsp maple syrup

1 Salt the skin of the pork belly and leave for 2 hours.

2 Preheat the oven to 130°C/250°F/gas mark ½. Rinse off the salt, pat the pork belly dry and place it, skin side up, in a roasting tin.

3 Mix the remaining ingredients together and smother all over the pork belly. Bake for 2½ hours then remove from the oven.

4 Turn your grill to medium high. Gently lift the pork belly into another roasting tin and place under the grill. Strain the cooking juices from the first tin into a saucepan and bring to a simmer on the stove top.

5 Turn the pork belly regularly to ensure it is grilled evenly and crisps up nicely.

6 Reduce the cooking liquid to a sticky syrup and brush it over the pork belly once it has crisped up. Carve and serve while hot.

1 Heat the vegetable oil in a large frying pan over a moderate heat. Add the onions, salt, tomato purée, garlic, ginger, spices and the 100g untoasted almonds, and fry until golden.

2 Add the stock and simmer gently for 5 minutes. Put into a blender and blend until smooth. Transfer to a deep frying pan and bring to a gentle simmer.

3 Add the remaining ingredients and bring back to a gentle simmer. Allow the vegetables to cook through, adding more water or stock if necessary. Adjust the seasoning and serve.

108

Chickpea and almond curry

SERVES 4

1 tbsp vegetable oil
1 medium onion, peeled
    and diced
½ tsp table salt
1 tbsp tomato purée
2 cloves garlic, peeled
    and crushed
80g fresh root ginger,
    peeled and finely diced
1 tsp turmeric
1 tsp curry powder
½ tsp garam masala
¼ tsp chilli powder
100g blanched whole almonds,
    plus 50g toasted
250ml chicken or vegetable stock
1 × 450g tin cooked chickpeas
1 × 400ml tin coconut milk
2 carrots, peeled and diced
1 large sweet potato, peeled
    and diced

Fragrant slow-baked chicken and rice

SERVES 4

2 cinnamon sticks
4 star anise
8 cardamom pods
1 tbsp cumin seeds
½ tsp coriander seeds
½ tsp ground turmeric
½ tsp coarsely ground black pepper
4 tbsp natural yogurt
1 tbsp tomato purée
8 chicken legs or thighs
4 tbsp vegetable oil
2 large onions, peeled and sliced
2 cloves garlic, peeled and crushed
2 bay leaves
200g basmati or jasmine rice
finely grated zest of 2 lemons
½ tsp table salt
1 litre chicken or vegetable stock

1 Dry-fry all the spices and the pepper, then remove 1 cinnamon stick, 2 star anise and 4 cardamom pods and set them aside. Grind the rest of the toasted spices in a spice grinder or with a pestle and mortar.

2 Mix the ground spices with the yogurt and tomato purée, then smother the mixture over the chicken pieces. Cover and refrigerate overnight.

3 Preheat the oven to 150°C/300°F/gas mark 2. Heat 2 tbsp of the oil in a large frying pan on a moderate to high heat. When hot, add the onions, garlic, bay leaves and the reserved whole spices.

4 Cook until the onions are coloured, then add the rice, lemon zest, salt and brown for a further 4 minutes. Pour into a large casserole dish.

5 Heat the remaining 2 tbsp oil in the frying pan and add the chicken pieces (only as many as will fit in the pan at one time). Brown well, then place the chicken on top of the rice in the casserole dish.

6 Deglaze the frying pan with the stock, then pour it over the chicken and rice.

7 Cover the entire dish with a lid or tinfoil and place in the oven for 2 hours.

8 Remove from the oven, allow to rest for 5 minutes, then remove the tinfoil and whole spices and serve.

Flatbread with lamb, couscous and tzatziki

SERVES 4

LAMB

2 tbsp soy sauce

1 tsp ground cumin

1 clove garlic, peeled and finely crushed

2 tbsp golden syrup

¼ bunch rosemary, leaves finely chopped

4 tbsp extra-virgin olive oil

2 lamb neck fillets (approximately 120g each)

25g unsalted butter

FLATBREADS

175g plain flour

1 tsp fast-action dried yeast

25ml toasted sesame oil

75ml tepid water

½ tsp table salt

½ tsp caster or granulated sugar

COUSCOUS

200ml chicken or vegetable stock, or water

125g couscous

1 tsp table salt

1 tsp cumin seeds

25g unsalted butter

2 medium onions, peeled and finely sliced

50g pine nuts, toasted

2 tbsp sesame oil

¼ bunch coriander, leaves chopped

TZATZIKI

300g Greek yogurt

2 tbsp mint sauce

¼ bunch mint, leaves chopped

½ cucumber, peeled, deseeded and grated

½ tsp table salt

1 For the lamb, combine the soy sauce, cumin, garlic, golden syrup and rosemary, and smother over the meat. Cover and refrigerate overnight.

2 For the flatbread dough, combine all the ingredients and knead for 5 minutes. Place in an oiled bowl, cover and leave somewhere warm for 30 minutes to double in volume.

3 When ready, place the dough on a floured surface and knead well. Divide it into eight balls, then roll each ball to a 4mm-thick circle and place between sheets of baking paper. Store in the fridge until required.

4 For the couscous, bring the stock or water to the boil. Meanwhile, put the couscous and a ½ tsp of the salt in a bowl, then pour the stock or water over. Mix well. Cover with clingfilm and set aside.

5 Heat a medium-sized frying pan over a moderate heat and toast the cumin seeds until fragrant, then add the butter, onions and remaining ½ tsp of salt, and cook for 15–20 minutes until the onions are lightly caramelized.

6 Fluff the couscous with a fork and stir in the onions, pine nuts, sesame oil and coriander.

7 For the tzatziki, combine all the ingredients and place in the fridge until ready to serve.

8 Heat a large frying pan and add the lamb with all the marinade. Brown well all over. Add the butter and cook until done to your taste. Set aside.

9 Clean the frying pan and place it back on a medium to high heat. Dry-fry the flatbreads on both sides for 1–2 minutes until they puff up. Serve immediately. Place all the dishes on the table and allow people to make up their own flatbreads.

Masala meatballs with coriander and coconut sauce

SERVES 4

MEATBALLS
2 tbsp cumin seeds
1 tsp turmeric
1 tsp ground coriander
¼ tsp chilli powder
½ tsp black mustard seeds
½ tsp ground cinnamon
1 medium onion, peeled and
    finely chopped
1 clove garlic, peeled and crushed
500g beef mince
1 tbsp tomato purée
½ tsp table salt

SAUCE
1 × 400ml tin coconut milk
½ bunch coriander, leaves
    chopped, stalks retained
80g fresh root ginger, peeled
    and chopped
1 tbsp brown sugar
½ tsp turmeric
½ tsp table salt
1 red chilli, deseeded and
    finely diced

2 tbsp vegetable oil

1 For the meatballs, place all the dried spices in a frying pan and dry-fry over a medium to high heat until fragrant. Blend them in a spice mill or crush with a pestle and mortar.

2 Stir the spice mixture, onion, garlic, mince, tomato purée and salt together. Form into small balls then place in the fridge.

3 For the sauce, put all the ingredients (including the coriander stalks but holding back half the coriander leaves) into a saucepan and simmer gently for 15 minutes. Pour into a blender and blend until smooth, then pass through a fine sieve.

4 Heat the vegetable oil in a frying pan over a moderate to high heat, then fry the meatballs. When well coloured and cooked through, remove them from the pan and lay them on paper towels. Garnish with the coriander leaves and serve with cocktail sticks and the dipping sauce.

Sweet and spicy tomato chicken curry

SERVES 4

2 tbsp vegetable oil
2 medium onions, peeled and
    finely diced
2 cloves garlic, peeled and crushed
80g fresh root ginger, peeled and
    finely chopped
1 stalk lemongrass, very finely
    chopped
2 red chillies, deseeded and
    finely chopped
500g tomato passata
300ml chicken or vegetable stock
½ tsp table salt
2 tbsp tomato purée
2 tbsp soft brown sugar
1 tsp turmeric
100g red lentils
3 cardamom pods
3 bay leaves
½ bunch coriander, leaves chopped
½ bunch basil, leaves chopped
2 large chicken breasts, diced

1 Heat 1 tbsp of the vegetable oil in a large frying pan over a moderate to high heat. Add the onions, garlic, ginger, lemongrass and chillies, and fry until coloured.

2 Add the remaining ingredients, except for the chicken, and mix well. Simmer for 15 minutes.

3 Heat the remaining tablespoon of vegetable oil in a separate frying pan. Season the chicken and fry until lightly browned all over. Add to the simmering curry base and cook for a further 10 minutes or until the chicken is well cooked through. Adjust the seasoning if necessary, then serve.

Spicy crusted squid with lemon chilli confit

SERVES 4

6 lemons
1 red chilli, seeds removed, finely
    chopped
50g caster or granulated sugar
200ml water
4 large squid tubes, tunics pulled
    off and sliced into 5mm rings
75g polenta (cornmeal)
25g plain flour
½ tsp coarsely ground black pepper
½ tsp table salt
¼ tsp smoked paprika
¼ tsp ground cumin
¼ tsp chilli powder
100ml vegetable oil
2 medium free-range eggs, beaten
1 spring onion, finely chopped
1 red chilli, finely chopped

1 To make the confit, slice four of the lemons into quarters lengthways, remove the seeds, then slice as finely as possible, with the skin on.

2 Put the lemon slices into a medium-sized saucepan with the chilli, sugar and water and place over a low heat until the sugar has dissolved.

3 Turn up the heat slightly and allow to simmer very gently, stirring occasionally, until you have a thick, sticky mixture. Set aside.

4 Grate the zest from the remaining two lemons and reserve. Squeeze out the juice and coat the squid rings with it, then refrigerate for 10 minutes.

5 Mix the polenta, flour, pepper, salt, spices and lemon zest together and set aside.

6 Add the oil to a large frying pan and allow to heat slowly. Drain the squid and pat dry with a paper towel.

7 Dip each squid ring into the flour mixture, then dust off, dip into the beaten egg, then back into the flour mixture.

8 Test the oil with a little of the egg: if it bubbles up to the surface then it is ready. Shallow fry the squid rings over a low heat until golden, then drain them on paper towels. Garnish with the spring onion and chilli, then serve immediately with the lemon chilli confit.

118

Hot and sour
sweet chilli crab

SERVES 4

4 tbsp vegetable oil
1 medium onion, peeled and diced
2 cloves garlic, peeled and crushed
2 stalks lemongrass, finely sliced
4 small crabs (body diameter 5–6cm),
    cut in half, dead man's fingers
    removed (ask your fishmonger
    to do this for you)
1 medium red chilli, finely diced
2 tbsp tamarind paste
2 tbsp tomato ketchup
4 tbsp soy sauce
2 tbsp hoisin sauce
1 tbsp fish sauce
½ tsp table salt
250ml chicken stock
½ bunch coriander, chopped

1 Heat the oil in a large non-stick saucepan over a moderate to high heat. Add the onion, garlic and lemongrass and fry until lightly coloured.

2 Add the crabs and colour well. Add the remaining ingredients, except the stock and coriander, and allow a sticky paste to form around the crab. Deglaze with the stock and place the lid on the pan, allowing the crabs to cook for 6 minutes.

3 Remove the lid, give everything a good stir and cook for a further 4 minutes at a gentle simmer.

4 Add the chopped coriander and serve, with some sticky rice, lobster crackers and fingerbowls.

Indonesian spiced seafood chowder

SERVES 4–6

16 whole raw prawns
1 tsp cumin seeds
1 tsp coriander seeds
1 tsp ground turmeric
2 star anise
4 tbsp vegetable oil
1 medium onion, peeled and
    finely sliced
2 cloves garlic, peeled and crushed
1 red chilli, finely diced
2 stalks lemongrass, finely sliced
1 large baking potato, peeled and
    finely sliced
1 tbsp tomato purée
2 litres chicken or vegetable stock
1 tsp table salt
½ bunch coriander, leaves chopped,
    stalks retained
1 tbsp peanut butter
1 × 400ml tin coconut milk
juice and finely grated zest of 1 lime
300g firm white fish (hake or sole,
    for example)
1 squid, tunic pulled off, cleaned
    and finely sliced into rings
    (tentacles included)
100g white crab meat (optional),
    picked through to remove
    any shell
2 tbsp roasted peanuts, roughly
    chopped

1 Twist the heads off the prawns and peel off their shells, but do not discard. Make a small incision at the top of the meaty part of each prawn going all the way down to the tail, then remove the small pipe and discard.

2 Heat a large saucepan, add the cumin and coriander seeds, the turmeric and star anise and dry-fry until fragrant.

3 Add 2 tbsp of the vegetable oil and the prawn shells and heads, and brown well. Add the onions, garlic, chilli and lemongrass, and continue to colour. When golden, add the potato, tomato purée, stock, a ½ tsp of the salt and the coriander stalks. Simmer gently for 30 minutes, then whiz in batches in a food processor or blender.

4 Strain through a fine sieve into a clean saucepan and place back on a moderate heat. Add a little of the hot soup to the peanut butter and mix well to form a paste, then return this to the soup and mix well.

5 Bring the soup to a rolling simmer and reduce by a third. Turn the heat down and add the coconut milk, lime juice and zest, and adjust the seasoning if necessary. Add the fish and poach gently until cooked through: about 5 minutes.

6 Heat the remaining vegetable oil in a large non-stick frying pan over a medium to high heat, season the prawns with the remaining ½ tsp of salt and fry them quickly until golden, then add to the soup. Season the squid and fry it in the same pan over the same heat until almost cooked through, then add to the soup.

7 Remove the fish from the soup, gently flake it, then return it to the pan. Add the crab, if using, and bring the soup back to a gentle simmer. Divide the soup between four to six bowls, garnishing with the chopped coriander leaves and the peanuts.

1 Put all the spices in a frying pan over a medium to high heat and dry-fry until fragrant. Remove them from the pan and crush using a pestle and mortar or spice grinder. Mix with the tea and store in an airtight jar.

2 To make the tea, use 1 tsp of the tea per person, steep well in boiling water for 2–3 minutes, then strain. Add milk and sugar if desired.

Masala tea

MAKES 75G

½ tsp cardamom pods
1 cinnamon stick
½ tsp cumin seeds
1 tsp whole cloves
1 tsp black pepper
1 tsp nutmeg, freshly grated
50g black tea (Assam or
    English Breakfast)

Slow-cooked spiced shoulder of lamb

SERVES 6–8

SPICE PASTE
½ tsp black peppercorns
2 tsp cayenne pepper
2 tsp black mustard seeds
3 cloves garlic, peeled and crushed
100g fresh root ginger, peeled
    and finely diced
1 medium onion, peeled and
    finely diced
4 tbsp flaked almonds
4 tsp desiccated coconut
1 nutmeg, finely grated
200g Greek yogurt
½ tsp salt
LAMB
1 medium-sized shoulder of lamb
    on the bone (approximately 2kg)
25g unsalted butter
3 cinnamon sticks
4 bay leaves
6 whole cloves
6 cardamom pods

1 For the spice paste, combine all the spices and crush, using a spice grinder or a pestle and mortar. Transfer to a blender, add the garlic, ginger, onion, almonds, coconut and nutmeg, and pulse briefly. Add the yogurt and salt and blend until smooth.

2 Using a sharp knife, score the flesh of the leg of lamb to make a criss-cross pattern 2–4mm deep. Smother the entire leg of lamb with the spice paste, cover and refrigerate for 2 hours.

3 Preheat the oven to 150°C/300°F/gas mark 2.

4 Put the butter and whole spices in a roasting tin large enough for the lamb and place in the oven for 10 minutes.

5 Remove the roasting tin and add the lamb. Cover with tinfoil, return to the oven and bake for 2 hours. Take it out of the oven and allow to rest for 10 minutes before carving.

SALAD BAR

I recall as a youngster going to those restaurants or bistros where they had salad bars. They were a real novelty, because you could actually choose whatever took your fancy as opposed to having to eat what was put in front of you.

This chapter is a homage to salads, vegetables and their accompaniments. Vegetables to me are one of the wonders of the world – something that, in their raw state, can look and taste so great that often they need little preparation or cooking to bring out their best. Seasonality is vital with vegetables, as it is only when they are ripened that they fulfil their natural potential and the flavours and texture meet perfection.

A lot of the salads in this chapter can be eaten as a meal in themselves, with others being a perfect addition to any part of a meal. Try the Vietnamese Beef Salad (page 137) for a zesty and tasty meal in summer, or the Jersey Royal, Pancetta and Pesto Salad (page 134) at the beginning of spring to comfort you with the knowledge that summer is on its way.

1 Place the vinegar, sugar and salt into a saucepan and bring to the boil. Stir until the sugar has dissolved, then remove from the heat and refrigerate until cold. Add the sardines and shallot and allow to marinate for at least 3 hours in the fridge.

2 To serve, take the sardines and shallot out of the marinade and arrange on plates with the peppers, tomatoes and ricotta.

3 Garnish with the olive oil, sea salt and basil cress.

124

Salad of soused sardines, piquillo peppers and ricotta

SERVES 2

100ml white wine vinegar
50g demerara sugar
pinch table salt
2 sardines, scaled, filleted and
    pin-boned (ask your fishmonger
    to do this for you)
1 banana shallot, peeled and sliced
    into 5mm rings
4 Piquillo peppers
6 sunblush tomatoes
4 tbsp fresh ricotta

GARNISH
extra-virgin olive oil
Maldon sea salt
basil cress (or small basil leaves)

Edamame, tofu, cashew and chilli noodle salad

SERVES 4

2 tbsp vegetable oil
75g cashew nuts
2 cloves garlic, peeled and crushed
1 onion, peeled and finely chopped
1 medium red chilli, finely sliced
6 tbsp oyster sauce
4 tbsp soy sauce
200g firm tofu, diced in large chunks
200g frozen Edamame beans, defrosted
200g egg noodles, precooked
2 tbsp toasted sesame oil
½ bunch coriander leaves, chopped

1 Heat the vegetable oil in a large frying pan or wok over a high heat. Add the cashew nuts and brown lightly.

2 Add the garlic, onion and chilli and fry for 1 minute. Add the oyster sauce and soy sauce and mix well.

3 Add the tofu, brown for a couple of minutes over the high heat, then add the Edamame beans.

4 Cook for 2 more minutes, then add the noodles and sesame oil and heat through. Garnish with the coriander and serve.

Seeded pumpkin salad

SERVES 4

1 small pumpkin, peeled and neatly
   diced into 2cm cubes
1 sweet potato, peeled and neatly
   diced into 2cm cubes
2 tbsp vegetable oil
2 tbsp linseed
100g pumpkin seeds
50g sunflower seeds
50g sesame seeds
1 tbsp soy sauce
½ bunch flat-leaf parsley, leaves chopped
¼ bunch tarragon, leaves chopped
3 stalks celery, peeled and finely diced
salt and coarsely ground black pepper

DRESSING
50ml sesame oil
50ml extra-virgin olive oil
1 tsp wasabi paste (use less if desired)
1 tbsp clear honey
50ml white wine or
   chardonnay vinegar
80g fresh root ginger,
   peeled and finely chopped

1 Preheat the oven to 180°C/350°F/gas mark 4. Toss the pumpkin and sweet potato in the vegetable oil, season well and place in a roasting tin in the oven for 20–30 minutes or until golden.

2 Heat a frying pan over a moderate heat, add the seeds and toast until golden brown. Add the soy sauce and shake until everything is evenly coated. Set aside.

3 For the dressing, whisk the sesame oil, olive oil, wasabi, honey, vinegar and ginger together until well combined.

4 Fold the roasted pumpkin and sweet potato together with the herbs and celery, and season to taste. Pour the dressing over and serve immediately.

Smoked paprika and sunblush tomato barley salad

SERVES 4

200g pearl barley
1 tbsp vegetable oil
1 onion, peeled and sliced
1 clove garlic, peeled and crushed
½ tsp table salt
1 tbsp sweet Spanish smoked paprika
2 tbsp tomato purée
100g sunblush tomatoes, chopped
50ml oil from the sunblush tomatoes,
    or extra-virgin olive oil
50g pitted black olives, sliced
½ tsp coarsely ground black pepper
¼ bunch flat-leaf parsley, leaves chopped

1 Place the barley in a saucepan of cold water and bring to a gentle boil. When the barley becomes tender (this should take around 25 minutes), rinse under cold running water and leave to drain in a sieve.

2 Put the vegetable oil in a medium-sized saucepan over a moderate heat. Add the onion, garlic and salt to the pan and cook until lightly golden.

3 Sprinkle in the paprika and cook for a few minutes longer. Add the tomato purée, tomatoes, oil, olives and pepper and mix well.

4 Place the drained barley into a large bowl and mix in the tomato dressing and parsley. Taste and adjust the seasoning if necessary.

Salad of confit of cod, leeks, blue cheese, prosciutto and parsley

SERVES 2 AS A STARTER

160g cod fillet (not too thick)
1 tsp rock salt
50ml extra-virgin olive oil,
    plus an extra 2 tbsp
6 baby leeks
50g your favourite blue cheese,
    crumbled
4 rashers prosciutto
¼ bunch flat-leaf parsley,
    leaves chopped
pinch Maldon sea salt

1 Sprinkle the cod with the rock salt, cover with clingfilm and refrigerate for 20 minutes. Remove and wash off all the salt, then pat dry.

2 Place the 50ml of oil in a small non-stick saucepan. Heat very gently until just above blood temperature (40°C). Remove from the heat and add the cod. Cover the cod directly with clingfilm and keep the pan in a warm place for 15 minutes, before removing the cod and gently flaking it. The heat of the oil is enough to cook and tenderize the cod.

3 Blanch the leeks in a pan of boiling water for 2 minutes, then refresh under cold water.

4 Arrange all the salad components on two plates and garnish with the 2 tbsp of olive oil and the sea salt.

1 Dry-fry the cumin, coriander, pepper and sesame seeds until fragrant, then mix with the chilli, ginger, mango chutney, vinegar and salt.

2 Gently toss the sweetcorn, carrot and cabbage together. Add the spiced dressing and coriander leaves and toss further until well combined.

NOTE: Use a dark mango chutney, as usually they have more flavour and aroma than the sweeter, yellow types.

131

Spiced sweetcorn and pickled ginger coleslaw

SERVES 4 AS A SIDE DISH

½ tsp ground cumin
½ tsp ground coriander
½ tsp coarsely ground black pepper
50g sesame seeds
1 medium red chilli, deseeded
    and very finely diced
50g pickled ginger, finely sliced
6 tbsp mango chutney (see note)
60ml vinegar from the pickled ginger
½ tsp table salt
400g sweetcorn kernels, frozen and
    defrosted or tinned and drained
2 carrots, peeled and julienned
½ pointed cabbage, white leaves
    only, finely shredded
½ bunch coriander, leaves
    finely chopped

Smoked baby beetroot, mascarpone and tarragon salad

SERVES 4

1 tbsp demerara sugar
1 tbsp uncooked rice
½ tbsp Lapsang Souchong tea leaves
250g cooked, lightly pickled baby
   beetroot
25g unsalted butter
100g walnuts
8 tbsp balsamic vinegar
4 tbsp extra-virgin olive oil
150g mascarpone
½ bunch tarragon leaves
½ tsp Maldon sea salt
½ tsp coarsely ground black pepper

1 Mix the sugar, rice and tea leaves together. Line a large baking dish with tinfoil and pour in the tea mixture.

2 Arrange the beetroot on a rack on top of the tea mixture. Cover the entire tray with tinfoil, ensuring there are no gaps through which the smoke could escape, and place over a moderate heat for 8 minutes.

3 Remove from the heat and allow to sit for 30 minutes without removing the tinfoil. When ready, dice the beetroot into 1cm cubes.

4 Heat the butter in a pan until foaming, then add the walnuts, season well and move continuously to allow them to colour evenly. When golden, pour into a colander to allow the excess butter to drain off.

5 Place the balsamic vinegar in a small saucepan and bring to a gentle simmer until it has reduced by two thirds. Add the oil to the pan and swirl to combine.

6 Place a large spoonful of mascarpone on each of four plates and smear it along the plate. Place the diced beetroot over the mascarpone and scatter with the tarragon, walnuts, salt and pepper. Drizzle with the balsamic dressing and serve.

Jersey royal, pancetta and pesto salad

SERVES 4

500g Jersey Royal potatoes,
   scrubbed
½ bunch basil
2 handfuls rocket
2 tbsp pine nuts, toasted
1 clove garlic, peeled and crushed
2 tbsp Parmesan, grated
½ tsp table salt
125ml extra-virgin olive oil
8 rashers pancetta
4 tbsp crème fraîche
coarsely ground black pepper

1 In a large saucepan, cover the potatoes with cold, seasoned water. Bring to the boil and allow to simmer until just tender when pierced with a sharp knife. Drain into a colander and allow to cool.

2 For the pesto, put the basil, rocket, pine nuts, garlic, Parmesan, salt and olive oil into a blender (or a container suitable for use with a stick blender) and blitz until combined.

3 Heat a frying pan over a moderate heat. When hot, add the pancetta and fry until slightly crispy, then remove from the pan.

4 To assemble the salad, stir half the pesto into half the crème fraîche and mix through the potatoes. Add the pancetta, then dollop the remaining pesto and crème fraîche on top, seasoned with coarsely ground black pepper.

Warm salad of broccoli, soy, ginger and sesame

SERVES 4

1 large head broccoli, broken
    into florets
100g sesame seeds
2 tbsp vegetable oil
200g green beans, trimmed
    and cut in half
4 tbsp soy sauce
2 tbsp toasted sesame oil
50g pickled ginger, chopped
2 tbsp pickling liquor from the ginger
¼ bunch coriander leaves, chopped

1 Bring a medium-sized saucepan of seasoned water to the boil. Add the broccoli and boil for 2 minutes. Remove from the heat and drain. Refresh under cold running water.

2 Toast the sesame seeds in a dry frying pan over a moderate heat until golden, then remove from the pan and set aside.

3 Add the vegetable oil to the frying pan and, when smoking, add the beans. Fry until slightly blackened in places but still crunchy, then add the broccoli, soy sauce and sesame oil.

4 Cook over a high heat until warmed through, then add the ginger and the 2 tbsp of the ginger pickling liquor. Sprinkle with the chopped coriander and serve.

Vietnamese beef salad

SERVES 4

BEEF
2 tbsp sesame oil
1 tbsp clear honey
2 tbsp soy sauce
400–600g rump steak
1 tbsp vegetable oil

DRESSING
4 tbsp sweet chilli sauce
2 tbsp rice wine vinegar
juice and finely grated zest
    of 1 lime
1 tsp fish sauce
½ stalk lemongrass, very finely
    chopped
80g fresh root ginger, peeled
    and finely chopped

SALAD
½ bulb fennel, very finely sliced
2 carrots, peeled and julienned
½ cucumber, peeled, deseeded
    and julienned
½ bunch coriander, leaves chopped
½ bunch mint, leaves chopped

50g peanuts, roasted and roughly
    chopped

1 Whisk the sesame oil, honey and soy sauce together, then pour over the beef and allow to marinate for at least 4 hours (or overnight).

2 Mix all the ingredients for the dressing together and set aside.

3 Heat the vegetable oil in a frying pan. When it is smoking, add the meat. Sear on both sides for a couple of minutes, then remove and allow to rest before slicing very thinly.

4 Roughly toss all the salad ingredients together with the dressing, then add the sliced beef and garnish with the peanuts.

Salad of quails' eggs, wholegrain mustard, prosciutto and caperberries

SERVES 4

125g sliced prosciutto
12 quails' eggs
1 medium free-range egg yolk
200ml vegetable oil
1 tsp white wine vinegar
2 tbsp wholegrain mustard
½ tsp table salt
4 large caperberries, thinly sliced
parsley or mustard cress
    to garnish

1 Preheat the oven to 180°C/350°F/gas mark 4. Chop one third of the prosciutto slices into strips, then place on a baking tray and bake until crisp – 5–10 minutes. Remove and allow to cool.

2 Bring a small saucepan of water to the boil. Gently place the quails' eggs in the water and cook for 3 minutes, then remove with a slotted spoon and place in a bowl of iced water. Allow to cool for 5 minutes, then remove and peel.

3 To make the mayonnaise, put the egg yolk in a deep bowl and whisk until pale. Drizzle the oil slowly into the yolk, whisking continuously. Once all the oil has been added, mix in the vinegar, mustard and salt.

4 To serve, arrange the remaining slices of prosciutto on four plates. Place three quails' eggs on top of each, then drizzle with the mayonnaise. Add the baked prosciutto strips (reserving one strip), then garnish with the caperberries and parsley or mustard cress. Chop the last strip of baked prosciutto very finely and sprinkle over the top.

BAKERY

I love walking into a bakery and being almost knocked over by the warm smell of freshly baked bread and buttery pastries, then impressed by the visual beauty of the rows of slices, cookies and pastries, all perfectly aligned, and the baskets filled with breads of all different shapes and flavours.

When I think of bakeries, I think of the amazing pâtisseries that line the boulevards in Paris. In France, it is an official title that can only be used by bakeries that employ a *maître pâtissier* (master pastry chef) and it carries the requirement that high standards be always met. I find it a struggle to walk past these shops, as I can almost taste the flaky, sweet wonders of the feather-light yet crispy pains au chocolat, still slightly warm from the oven. Teamed with a strong coffee, they are pure bliss!

I love recreating that comforting smell of baking at home, and find the light approach it needs another of its relaxing and soothing qualities. Given that I also have a rather sweet tooth, to me there is nothing better than a large pot of Yorkshire tea and any one of the sweet treats in this chapter. As a must, I urge you to try the Jaffa Cakes, Custard Squares and Chocolate and Blackberry Jammy Dodgers (pages 158, 163 and 170) – and last but not least the Manchester Tart Slice (page 155). I used to have a version of this treat when I was a boy at school and it still hasn't lost its charm!

1 Preheat the oven to 180°C/350°F/gas mark 4 and grease a 12-hole muffin tin.

2 Place the flour, baking powder, salt, pepper, mustard seeds and half the cheese in a large mixing bowl.

3 Mix the eggs, milk, mustard, onion, garlic, parsley and half the pickle together. Add to the dry ingredients and mix lightly until just combined.

4 Mix the remaining pickle and remaining cheese together separately. Half fill each mould in the muffin tin with the flour mixture, then place one twelfth of the cheese and pickle mixture on top of each one. Top with the remaining muffin mixture. Sprinkle with the sesame seeds and bake for 15–20 minutes, or until a skewer inserted comes out clean. Remove from the oven and allow the muffins to cool in the tin.

142

Cheese and pickle muffins

MAKES 12 LARGE MUFFINS

1 tsp vegetable oil, for greasing
250g plain flour
2 tsp baking powder
1 tsp table salt
½ tsp coarsely ground black pepper
1 tsp black mustard seeds
100g Cheddar cheese, grated
3 medium free-range eggs
250ml semi-skimmed or whole milk
1 tsp English mustard
1 small onion, peeled and finely diced
1 clove garlic, peeled and crushed
½ bunch flat-leaf parsley, leaves chopped
150g pickle of your choice
2 tbsp sesame seeds

Sundried tomato and sweetcorn muffins

MAKES 12 LARGE MUFFINS

1 tsp vegetable oil, for greasing
250g plain flour
50g polenta (cornmeal)
2 tsp baking powder
1 tsp cumin seeds, toasted
1 tsp table salt
½ tsp freshly milled black pepper
50g Cheddar cheese, grated
3 medium free-range eggs
100g sundried tomatoes in oil,
    drained and chopped
½ bunch coriander, leaves chopped
¼ bunch tarragon, leaves chopped
250g frozen and defrosted or tinned
    and drained sweencorn kernels
100ml oil from the sundried tomatoes,
    or extra-virgin olive oil
250ml semi-skimmed or whole milk
2 tbsp sesame seeds

1 Preheat the oven to 180°C/350°F/ gas mark 4 and grease a 12-hole muffin tin.

2 Place the flour, polenta, baking powder, cumin seeds, salt, pepper and cheese in a large bowl.

3 Mix the eggs, sundried tomatoes, oil, herbs, sweetcorn and milk together, then add to the dry ingredients and mix lightly until just combined.

4 Fill the muffin moulds, sprinkle with the sesame seeds, then place in the oven for 15–20 minutes or until a skewer inserted comes out clean. Leave the muffins to cool in the tin.

144

Nutmeg and custard cream 'yo-yos'

MAKES 12

BISCUITS
150g unsalted butter, softened,
    plus extra for greasing
40g icing sugar, sieved
2 tbsp custard powder
165g plain flour
1 nutmeg
FILLING
80g unsalted butter, softened
75g icing sugar, sieved
2 tbsp custard powder

1 Preheat the oven to 165°C/325°F/gas mark 3.

2 For the biscuits, cream the butter and icing sugar together until light and fluffy. Sieve the custard powder and flour together, then mix into the creamed butter.

3 Roll the dough into a sausage shape, approximately 4cm in diameter, and wrap it tightly in clingfilm. Refrigerate for 30 minutes until firm, then cut into 24 slices and lay them on a baking tray lined with lightly greased baking paper.

4 Grate the nutmeg over the top of the biscuits, then bake for 15–20 minutes until pale golden. Leave to cool on the baking tray.

5 For the filling, cream all the ingredients together until light and fluffy. When the biscuits are cold, sandwich them together with the filling and leave to set for 30 minutes. Store in an airtight container for up to 3 days.

Olive, feta and herb muffins

MAKES 12 LARGE MUFFINS

1 tsp vegetable oil, for greasing
250g plain flour
2 tsp baking powder
½ tsp table salt
½ tsp coarsely ground black pepper
40g Cheddar cheese, grated
3 medium free-range eggs
7 tbsp semi-skimmed or whole milk
50ml extra-virgin olive oil
100g black or green pitted olives, sliced
¼ bunch tarragon, leaves chopped
¼ bunch flat-leaf parsley, leaves chopped
¼ bunch thyme leaves
100g feta cheese
50g cream cheese
2 tbsp pumpkin seeds

1 Preheat the oven to 180°C/350°F/gas mark 4 and grease a 12-hole muffin tin.

2 Mix the flour, baking powder, salt and pepper together with the Cheddar cheese in a large mixing bowl.

3 Stir the eggs, 2 tbsp of the milk, the oil, olives and herbs together, then add to the dry ingredients and mix lightly until just combined.

4 Mix together the feta, cream cheese and remaining milk to form a paste. Half fill each mould in the muffin tin with the muffin mixture, place one twelfth of the feta mixture on top of each one, then top with the remaining muffin mixture.

5 Sprinkle with pumpkin seeds, then place in the oven for 15–20 minutes or until a skewer inserted comes out clean. Leave the muffins to cool in the tin.

148

Sundried tomato and feta stuffed mini loaves

MAKES 8

DOUGH
250g plain flour, plus extra
    for dusting
2 tsp fast-action dried yeast
½ tsp table salt
½ tsp caster or granulated sugar
30ml extra-virgin olive oil,
    plus extra for greasing
125ml water

FILLING
100g sundried tomatoes in oil,
    drained and finely chopped
100g feta cheese, crumbled
50g Cheddar cheese, grated
¼ bunch basil, leaves chopped
¼ medium onion, peeled
    and finely chopped
½ tsp coarsely ground black pepper

1 In a large bowl, mix together all the ingredients for the dough and knead well for 5 minutes. Place in an oiled bowl, cover and leave somewhere warm to double in volume for 30 minutes.

2 Mix together the ingredients for the filling and set aside.

3 Preheat the oven to 180°C/350°F/ gas mark 4 and grease eight 4cm × 8cm × 4cm mini loaf tins or an 8-hole muffin tin.

4 When the dough has doubled in size, tip it out on to a floured surface, knead for another 5 minutes and divide into eight balls.

5 Divide one of the dough balls into five and roll out small circles approximately 5cm in diameter.

6 Place half a teaspoonful of the tomato and cheese mixture in the centre of each circle, then gather the edges together so that they are sealed, forming a little pouch. Place in one of the loaf tins. Repeat with the remaining four discs of dough and place in the same tin, on top of the first pouch.

7 Repeat steps 5 and 6 with the remaining dough balls. Bake the loaves for 15–20 minutes until a light golden colour. Remove from the tins and leave to cool on a wire rack.

Spiced chocolate cornflake cookies

MAKES 12 LARGE COOKIES

COOKIES
150g unsalted butter, softened
125g caster or granulated sugar
½ nutmeg, freshly grated
½ tsp ground cinnamon
½ tsp ground ginger
300g plain flour
30g cocoa powder
150g cornflakes
50g dark chocolate (minimum
    60% cocoa solids), broken
    into chunks
ICING
25g unsalted butter
50g dark chocolate (minimum
    60% cocoa solids)
50g cocoa powder
50g icing sugar, sieved

white chocolate, melted,
    to decorate (optional)

1 Preheat the oven to 180°C/350°F/gas mark 4.

2 Cream the butter and sugar with the spices until pale and fluffy. Sieve the flour and cocoa powder together and fold into the butter mix. Add the cornflakes and chocolate chunks and mix well.

3 Divide the mixture into twelve balls and flatten each one on a baking tray lined with lightly greased baking paper. Bake in the oven for 10–15 minutes until lightly golden. Cool on a wire rack.

4 To make the icing, melt the butter and chocolate together in a bowl placed over a pan of simmering water. Sieve the cocoa powder and icing sugar into the bowl and mix well.

5 Spread the icing over the cooled cookies. If you wish, drizzle melted white chocolate over the top, using a fork.

Baked ricotta, honey and spiced cherry tart

MAKES ONE 20CM TART

PASTRY

75g unsalted butter, at room
   temperature
40g icing sugar, sieved
pinch table salt
1 medium free-range egg, beaten
150g plain flour, plus extra
   for dusting

FILLING

8 tbsp clear honey
½ tsp coarsely ground black pepper
½ tsp ground cinnamon
½ nutmeg, freshly grated
¼ tsp ground cardamom
400g fresh cherries, halved
   and stoned
50ml cherry brandy or Kirsch
250g fresh ricotta
150g crème fraîche
100ml semi-skimmed
   or whole milk
2 medium free-range eggs

1 For the pastry, cream the butter and icing sugar together in a bowl until pale and fluffy. Add the salt and egg and mix well. Add the flour and mix until the dough just comes together (be careful not to over-work it).

2 Turn the dough out on to a floured surface and shape into a ball. Wrap it in clingfilm and refrigerate for 30 minutes until firm. Place a tart ring 20cm in diameter and 3–4cm deep in the freezer to chill.

3 Remove the pastry from the fridge and dip it in flour, then place on a sheet of baking paper. Roll it into a circle approximately 27cm in diameter, then return it to the fridge for 2 minutes.

4 Put the chilled tart ring on a square of baking paper on a baking tray. Line the inside of the tart ring with the pastry, letting it hang over the top. Press it firmly into the base and sides. Refrigerate for 20 minutes and preheat the oven to 165°C/325°F/gas mark 3.

5 Line the pastry with baking paper and fill with baking beans or rice. Bake blind for 25 minutes. Remove the beans or rice and paper, then cook for a further 8 minutes. Remove and set aside.

6 Turn the oven down to 130°C/250°F/gas mark ½. Place 4 tbsp of the honey in a pan over a low heat until it turns a deep golden colour. Add the spices and infuse for 1 minute, then add the cherries and cherry brandy or Kirsch. Mix well and cook for 2 minutes, then pour the mixture into a colander set over a bowl to catch the juices.

7 Meanwhile, whisk the ricotta, crème fraîche, milk, eggs and remaining honey together until smooth. Place the liquid from the cherries in a saucepan over a moderate heat. Simmer gently and reduce to a glaze, then mix with the cherries.

8 Spread the cherries over the bottom of the pastry case, then pour over the ricotta mixture. Bake for 25–30 minutes until there is only a slight wobble in the centre. Cool completely before serving.

Spiced apple crumble slice

MAKES 12 SLICES

APPLES

6 Granny Smith apples, peeled,
cored and sliced

100g caster or granulated sugar

SHORTBREAD BASE

75g unsalted butter, softened,
plus extra for greasing

40g caster or granulated sugar

1 medium free-range egg, beaten

2 tbsp semi-skimmed or whole milk

75g plain flour

50g wholemeal flour

½ tsp baking powder

25g wheatgerm

CRUMBLE

50g rolled oats

40g wholemeal flour

15g wheatgerm

50g walnuts, chopped

pinch table salt

50g caster or granulated sugar

1 tsp ground cinnamon

½ tsp ground ginger

½ nutmeg, freshly grated

60g unsalted butter

1 Place the apples in a saucepan with the sugar. Cover and set over a low heat until the juice begins to come out of the apples. Slightly increase the heat and cook until the apples are soft, then set aside to cool.

2 Preheat the oven to 165°C/325°F/gas mark 3.

3 For the shortbread base, cream together the butter and sugar, add the egg and milk, then mix in the flours, baking powder and wheatgerm. Spread over the bottom of a greased cake tin (approximately 20cm × 20cm × 5cm) and bake in the oven for 10 minutes. Leave to cool in the tin.

4 Make the crumble by mixing all the dry ingredients together. Put the butter in a small saucepan, melt over a moderate heat, then pour it over the dry ingredients and mix together.

5 Spread the apple over the shortbread base, then sprinkle the crumble mix over the top. Bake for 10–15 minutes until lightly golden. Serve warm with vanilla ice cream.

Pumpkin seed and thyme oatcakes

MAKES 12

120g rolled oats
120g wholemeal flour,
    plus extra for dusting
1 tsp bicarbonate of soda
½ tsp table salt
20g thyme leaves
50g pumpkin seeds,
    toasted and chopped
100ml boiling water
2 tbsp extra-virgin olive oil,
    plus extra for greasing
Maldon sea salt, for sprinkling

1 Preheat the oven to 165°C/325°F/gas mark 3. Mix the rolled oats, flour, bicarbonate of soda, salt, thyme and pumpkin seeds together.

2 Pour the water and olive oil over and mix to a smooth dough.

3 Roll out on a well-floured surface to a thickness of half a centimetre and cut into rounds using a ring-cutter. Sprinkle with a little sea salt, then bake on a greased tray for 10–15 minutes until lightly golden. Leave to cool on a wire rack.

155

Manchester tart slice

MAKES 12 SLICES

BASE
150g unsalted butter, softened
100g caster or granulated sugar
1 medium free-range egg, beaten
175g plain flour mixed with 1 tsp
    baking powder

FILLING
200g raspberry jam
2 tbsp caster or granulated sugar
2 tbsp rum
2 tbsp unsalted butter
4 ripe bananas, sliced

CUSTARD
750ml semi-skimmed or whole milk
4 medium free-range egg yolks
4 tbsp caster sugar
5 tbsp custard powder

TOPPING
50g desiccated coconut

1 Heat the oven to 180°C/350°F/gas mark 4. Grease a 30cm × 20cm × 5cm baking tin and line with baking paper.

2 For the base, cream the butter and sugar until fluffy. Beat in the egg, then fold in the flour and baking powder.

3 Flatten the mixture into the tin and bake for 10–15 minutes until lightly golden. Remove from the oven and allow to cool in the tin for 30 minutes.

4 For the filling, first spread the raspberry jam over the cooled base.

5 Heat a frying pan over a high heat. Add the sugar to the pan and melt to form a caramel, swirling all the time. Add the rum, then whisk in the butter. Add the banana slices and toss gently until coated and caramelized. Layer on top of the raspberry jam, then place the tin in the fridge for 30 minutes.

6 For the custard, put the milk in a saucepan, bring to the boil, then reduce the heat. In a bowl, whisk the egg yolks, sugar and custard powder together until smooth. Pour a little of the hot milk on to this mixture, whisk well, then add it back to the hot milk. Cook the custard over a low heat, stirring constantly, until the mixture is very thick.

7 Pour the custard on top of the bananas in the tin, sprinkle with the coconut, then refrigerate for 30–40 minutes until set.

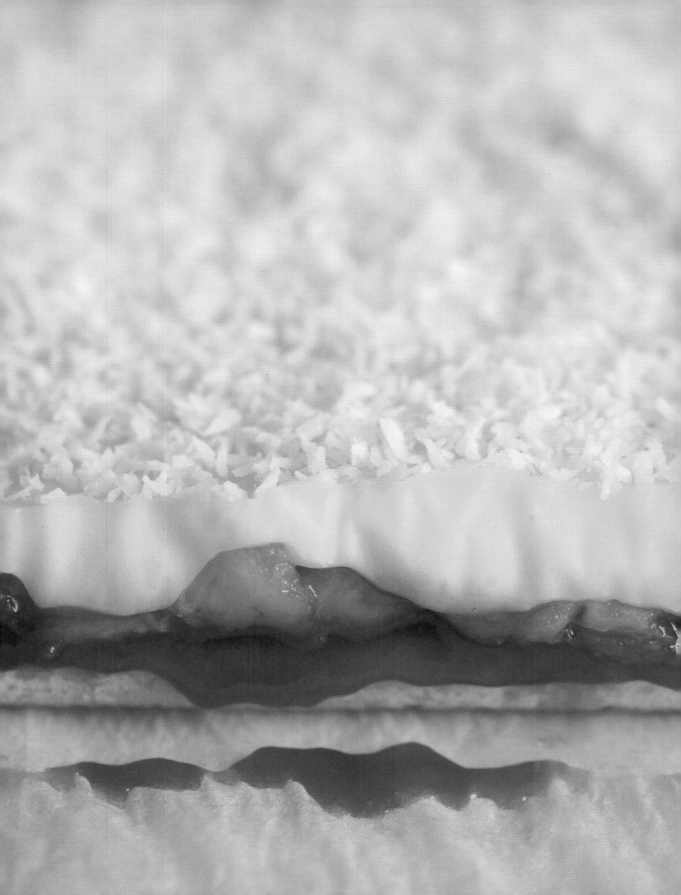

Jaffa cakes

MAKES 12

1 medium free-range egg, sat in
    warm water for 10 minutes
40g caster sugar
1 tbsp unsalted butter, plus extra
    for greasing
60g plain flour
20g ground almonds
12 tsp Seville orange marmalade
75g dark chocolate (minimum
    60% cocoa solids), broken
    into chunks

1 Preheat the oven to 180°C/350°F/gas mark 4 and grease a 12-hole muffin tin.

2 Break the warmed egg into a mixing bowl, add the sugar, then whisk on high speed for 10 minutes until light and fluffy.

3 Melt the butter in a saucepan over a moderate heat, add to the egg, then gently fold in the flour and ground almonds. Spoon into the moulds and bake for 10 minutes or until a skewer inserted comes out clean.

4 Allow the cakes to cool on a wire rack, then cut each one in half through the middle, forming a base and a lid. Scoop out a small piece of each base and fill with a teaspoon of marmalade, then put the lids back on top.

5 Melt the chocolate in a bowl placed over a pan of simmering water until smooth. Place a tray lined with baking paper on your work surface then, using a fork, dip the cakes in the chocolate, then set them on the paper.

6 When you have dipped all the cakes, put them in the fridge to set for 10–15 minutes. As a garnish, decorate with small pieces of peel from the marmalade.

Lemon shortbread with tangy lemon crunch

MAKES 24 BISCUITS

250g unsalted butter, softened,
    plus extra for greasing
125g icing sugar, sieved
juice and zest of 4 lemons
125g cornflour
250g plain flour
4 tbsp granulated sugar

1 Preheat the oven to 165°C/325°F/gas mark 3.

2 Cream the butter, icing sugar and lemon zest until pale and fluffy. Sieve the cornflour and flour together, then fold into the butter mixture.

3 Mix until smooth, then divide in two. Form each piece into a rectangular log 4cm × 4cm, so that when you slice it the biscuits will be square. Cover with clingfilm and refrigerate for 30 minutes until slightly firm.

4 Once the logs have firmed up, take them out of the fridge and cut them into 1cm-thick slices. Place them on a greased baking tray and bake for 15–20 minutes or until pale golden in colour.

5 Remove from the oven, brush each biscuit with a liberal amount of lemon juice, then sprinkle sugar over each biscuit. Return them to the oven and bake for a further 4 minutes. Leave to cool on a wire rack.

Gingercrunch slice

MAKES 16 SLICES

BASE

125g unsalted butter, softened,
   plus extra for greasing
100g caster sugar
3 tsp ground ginger
½ tsp ground cinnamon
¼ nutmeg, freshly grated
180g plain flour mixed with
   ½ tsp baking powder

TOPPING

150g unsalted butter, softened
4 tbsp golden syrup
100g fresh root ginger, peeled
   and very finely crushed
225g icing sugar, sieved

1 Preheat the oven to 180°C/350°F/gas mark 4. Grease a 30cm × 20cm × 5cm baking tin and line with baking paper.

2 For the base, cream the butter, sugar and spices until pale and fluffy. Fold in the flour and baking powder.

3 Put the mixture into the tin in an even layer and bake for 10–15 minutes until lightly golden. Remove from the oven and allow to cool slightly.

4 Place the topping ingredients in a saucepan, bring to a gentle simmer and continue simmering for 5 minutes, stirring continuously. Beat well, then pour the mixture over the base and leave to cool in the fridge for 30 minutes. When cold, heat a knife under hot water and cut into slices.

163

Custom squares

MAKES 16 SMALL SQUARES

PASTRY
2 sheets puff pastry rolled to
    25cm × 25cm × 3mm thickness
2 tbsp clear honey
unsalted butter, for greasing

CUSTARD
1 litre semi-skimmed or whole milk
4 medium free-range egg yolks
75g caster or granulated sugar
6 tbsp custard powder

ICING
150g icing sugar
2 tbsp boiling water
25g unsalted butter

1 Preheat the oven to 180°C/350°F/gas mark 4. Grease a baking tray and line it with greased baking paper.

2 Prick the pastry all over with a fork, then lay both sheets on the baking paper. Bake for 8–12 minutes until golden. Brush each sheet with honey and place in the oven for a further 4 minutes. Remove and set aside to cool.

3 For the custard, put the milk in a saucepan over a moderate heat and bring to the boil gently, then reduce the heat. Whisk the egg yolks, sugar and custard powder together until smooth. Pour a little of the hot milk on to this mixture, whisk well, then add it back to the hot milk. Whisk together, then cook over a low heat until the mixture is thick, stirring constantly.

4 Remove from the heat and pour the custard into a large mixing bowl. Place this over another bowl full of ice and whisk until the custard is merely tepid.

5 Spread the custard neatly on to one sheet of the pastry (honey side up) and sandwich the other sheet (honey side down) on top, scraping the edges to form a square. Refrigerate for 30–40 minutes until set.

6 For the icing, mix the icing sugar with the water. Melt the butter in a small saucepan over a moderate heat, then combine with the icing sugar and water, and whisk well. Spread the icing over the cooled pastry and smooth with a knife heated under hot water if necessary. Allow to chill in the fridge for a further 20 minutes, then cut into squares using a sharp, serrated knife.

Honeycomb biscuits

MAKES 12-16

180g plain flour
5 tbsp clear honey
75g caster sugar
100g unsalted butter
2 tbsp semi-skimmed
    or whole milk
1 tsp bicarbonate of soda

1 Preheat the oven to 180°C/350°F/gas mark 4. Place the flour in a mixing bowl and set aside.

2 Put 4 tbsp of the honey in a saucepan over a moderate heat and allow to bubble until it turns a deep golden colour. Add the sugar, butter and milk, and stir well until the sugar has dissolved and everything is completely combined.

3 Remove from the heat and add the bicarbonate of soda, mixing well. Pour on to the flour and mix together until just combined.

4 Roll the mixture into a sausage shape with a 5cm diameter and wrap in clingfilm. Refrigerate for 30 minutes until just firm.

5 Line a baking tray with baking paper. Slice the dough into 1cm slices and set these on the baking paper. Place in the oven for 10 minutes.

6 Remove from the oven and drizzle the biscuits with the remaining honey, then bake for a further 5–10 minutes until lightly golden. Leave to cool on a wire rack.

166

Chocolate-dipped gingernuts

MAKES 16

125g unsalted butter, softened,
    plus extra for greasing
25g caster or granulated sugar
50g soft brown sugar
3 tbsp golden syrup
1 tsp bicarbonate of soda
1 tbsp boiling water
75g stem ginger in syrup,
    finely chopped
2 tsp ground ginger
250g plain flour
¼ tsp table salt
75g dark chocolate (minimum
    60% cocoa solids), broken
    into chunks

1 Preheat the oven to 180°C/350°F/gas mark 4. Cream the butter, sugars and golden syrup until pale and fluffy.

2 Mix the bicarbonate of soda and boiling water together, then add to the butter mixture with the stem ginger. Lastly, mix in the ground ginger, flour and salt.

3 Divide the dough into sixteen balls, place them on a greased baking tray and gently flatten with the palm of your hand. Bake in the oven for 15–20 minutes until lightly golden. Remove from the oven and allow to cool on a wire rack.

4 Melt the chocolate in a bowl placed over a pan of gently simmering water. Place a tray lined with baking paper on your work surface. Dip one half of each biscuit into the chocolate, shake off the excess, then place on the paper to set.

Chocolate chunk cookies with cinnamon

MAKES 15

125g unsalted butter, softened,
    plus extra for greasing
50g caster sugar
4 tbsp condensed milk
pinch table salt
2 tsp ground cinnamon
180g plain flour
1 tsp baking powder
50g dark chocolate (minimum
    60% cocoa solids), cut into
    small chunks

1 Preheat the oven to 165°C/325°F/gas mark 3. Cream the butter, sugar, condensed milk, salt and cinnamon together until pale and fluffy.

2 In another bowl, mix the flour, baking powder and chocolate together, then add to the butter mixture.

3 Combine well, then divide the mixture into fifteen balls and place on a greased baking tray. Gently flatten them with the palm of your hand, then bake in the oven for 15–20 minutes until lightly golden. Remove from the oven and leave to cool on a wire rack.

Caramel chocolate cookies

MAKES 15

COOKIES
100g unsalted butter, softened,
   plus extra for greasing
125g caster or granulated sugar
1 medium free-range egg
175g plain flour
1 tsp baking powder
CARAMEL
½ × 397g tin condensed milk
3 tbsp demerara sugar
50g unsalted butter
1 tsp golden syrup
TOPPING
125g dark chocolate (minimum
   60% cocoa solids), broken
   into chunks

1 For the cookies, cream the butter and sugar together until pale and fluffy. Add the egg, mix well, then add the flour and baking powder, mixing until just combined.

2 Shape the dough into a log about 3cm in diameter, wrap it tightly in clingfilm to form a perfect sausage shape and refrigerate for 30 minutes.

3 When the cookie dough is firm, preheat the oven to 165°C/325°F/gas mark 3. Slice 5mm rounds off the log and place them on a well-greased baking tray. Bake in the oven for 10–15 minutes or until a pale golden colour.

4 For the caramel, place all the ingredients in a small saucepan over a low heat. Stir regularly and allow the mixture to thicken, being very careful not to let it catch. When you can see the caramel setting on the side of the pan, it is ready.

5 Transfer to a shallow container, cover by laying clingfilm directly on the surface, and leave to cool for 30 minutes.

6 When cool, divide the caramel and roll it into fifteen balls, place one ball on each cookie, then shape to form a flattened dome on top of each cookie.

7 Melt the chocolate in a bowl placed over a pan of simmering water. Place a cookie on a slotted spoon and dip into the chocolate. Shake off the excess and gently place the cookie on a sheet of baking paper. Repeat with the others and, when finished, put them in the fridge to set for 30 minutes.

Chocolate and blackberry jammy dodgers

MAKES 12

SHORTBREAD
200g plain flour, plus a little extra
100g icing sugar
150g unsalted butter, diced
    and chilled
1 medium free-range egg yolk

JAM
300g frozen blackberries
100g water
175g jam sugar (contains pectin
    to help the jam set)

50g milk chocolate, broken
    into chunks

1 Sieve the flour and icing sugar together, then rub in the butter with your fingers until it disappears. Add the egg yolk and mix until just combined. Wrap the dough in clingfilm and chill in the fridge for 20 minutes.

2 Preheat the oven to 165°C/325°F/gas mark 3. Dip the shortbread dough in flour, then roll it out on baking paper to a thickness of 2mm. Transfer to a baking tray and bake for 5 minutes, then remove and cut out twenty-four circles using a 5cm-diameter ring-cutter. Using a 2cm-diameter ring-cutter, cut out the centre of twelve of the biscuits. Place all the biscuits back in the oven for 4–6 minutes or until lightly golden. Remove and cool on a wire rack.

3 For the jam, place the blackberries and water in a medium-sized saucepan over a moderate to high heat and stir continuously until dissolved. Cook down to a pulp, then add the sugar and stir until dissolved.

4 Boil rapidly for 5 minutes, stirring occasionally to ensure the jam does not catch on the bottom of the pan, then transfer to a shallow container and place in the fridge to cool quickly.

5 Melt the chocolate in a bowl placed over a pan of gently simmering water. Place a tray lined with baking paper on your work surface. Spread the underside of the biscuits without the hole with a thin layer of chocolate, then lay them chocolate side down on the paper and refrigerate for 25 minutes. Place the other twelve biscuits on a sheet of baking paper on another tray. Using a fork, line the biscuits with thin streams of chocolate. Refrigerate for 20 minutes.

6 To assemble, spread a heaped teaspoon of jam on to the chocolate side of each biscuit, then place a biscuit with a hole on top and squeeze gently together. Allow to set in the fridge for at least 2 hours before serving.

172

Chocolate and hazelnut meringues

MAKES 12 DOUBLE MERINGUES

4 medium free-range egg whites
100g caster sugar
100g icing sugar, sieved
50g toasted hazelnuts, finely chopped
50g dark chocolate (minimum 60%
    cocoa solids), finely chopped
6 tbsp Nutella
1 tbsp clear honey
1 tbsp unsalted butter, softened

1 Preheat the oven to 90°C/195°F/gas mark ¼ or lowest possible setting.

2 Whisk the egg whites until stiff peaks form, then add the caster sugar and whisk until thick and glossy. Fold in the icing sugar followed by the hazelnuts and chocolate.

3 Line a baking tray with baking paper and, using a piping bag, pipe twenty-four 4cm-diameter meringues on to it. Place in the oven for 5 minutes, then turn the oven off and leave the meringues inside for 1 hour. Remove them from the oven and allow to cool.

4 For the filling, combine the Nutella, honey and butter until smooth.

5 Using a spoon or a piping bag, spread the filling over twelve of the cooled meringues, then sandwich the remaining twelve on top. Store in an airtight container for up to 2 days.

Bitter chocolate, cranberry and macadamia florentines

MAKES 12

100g unsalted butter, softened
125g caster sugar
4 tbsp golden syrup
75g plain flour
125g macadamia nuts
60g dried cranberries
100g dark chocolate (minimum
    70% cocoa solids), broken
    into chunks

1 Preheat the oven to 180°C/350°F/gas mark 4.

2 Cream the butter and sugar until light and fluffy, then add the golden syrup and mix well. Fold in the flour, then the nuts and cranberries.

3 Place 12 tablespoonfuls of mixture on to a baking tray lined with baking paper, leaving 3–5cm between each spoonful for the mix to spread.

4 Flatten each circle as much as possible using a palette knife, then bake for 10 minutes or until golden brown. Allow to cool on the tray.

5 While the Florentines are cooling, melt the chocolate in a bowl placed over a pan of gently simmering water. Using a fork, drizzle the chocolate liberally over the Florentines. Place the tray in the fridge to set if necessary.

Brioche pillows with spiced apple and custard

MAKES 8

DOUGH
200g plain flour
1 tbsp caster sugar
1 tsp fast-action dried yeast
2 medium free-range eggs
4 tbsp semi-skimmed or whole milk
½ tsp table salt
75g unsalted butter, softened

SPICED APPLE
4 Granny Smith apples, peeled,
    cored and sliced
50g caster or granulated sugar
½ tsp ground cinnamon
½ nutmeg, freshly grated
½ tsp ground ginger

CUSTARD
200ml semi-skimmed or whole milk
2 medium free-range egg yolks
1 tbsp caster or granulated sugar
1 tbsp custard powder

TOPPING
1 medium free-range egg yolk
½ nutmeg, freshly grated

1 Place the flour, sugar, yeast, eggs, milk and salt in the bowl of an electric mixer with a dough hook. Mix on low until a smooth dough is formed. Increase the speed until the dough begins to leave the side of the bowl, then add the butter and continue to mix on high until well combined. Cover the bowl and leave in a warm place until the dough has doubled in volume.

2 Meanwhile, put the apples, sugar and spices into a saucepan. Cover and place over a low heat until the juice begins to come out of the apples. Increase the heat slightly and cook until the apples are tender and thick, then set aside.

3 For the custard, bring the milk to the boil. In a bowl, whisk the egg yolks, sugar and custard powder together, then pour the hot milk over. Return the mixture to the pan and stir over a very low heat until the custard is really thick. Strain through a fine sieve into a shallow container. Cover the custard with clingfilm placed directly on the surface and refrigerate for 30 minutes.

4 When the brioche dough has doubled in volume, preheat the oven to 165°C/325°F/gas mark 3. Turn the dough on to a floured surface and knead for a couple of minutes.

5 Cut the dough into eight pieces and roll each piece into a rectangle half a centimetre thick. Spoon one eighth of the apple mixture on to one third of the dough, then fold the dough over to form an apple-filled pocket. Spoon one eighth of the custard on to the last third of the dough and fold this on top of the apple-filled pocket. Pinch the sides to contain the fillings. Place the brioche pillow on a baking tray lined with baking paper. When you have finished all the pillows, allow them to rest for 5 minutes, then brush them with a little egg yolk and sprinkle with nutmeg.

6 Bake in the oven for 15–20 minutes until a light golden colour, then leave to cool on a wire rack.

PUDS

Puddings encompass many of the most important aspects of cookery. And as the finale of a great-tasting meal, you must have something special. In the restaurant, my desserts are beautiful both to the eye and to the palate. To me, however, taste is more important than the way the food looks. Of course it must also be visually appealing, but to quote a cliché, beauty is only skin deep.

The puddings in this chapter vary in complexity, so pick and choose what suits your tastes, your skills and your desired outcome. There are some unusual and interesting dishes that we created as *Nutmeg & Custard* evolved. There are also some staples from the restaurant that I felt needed to be shared with you.

I have included our version of Raspberry Eton Mess (page 188) – quite the opposite of a mess, and it tastes fabulous. The Chargrilled Bananas with Bitter Chocolate and Toasted Marshmallow Ice Cream (page 178) are also an old-time childhood favourite of mine in a slightly modernized adult version and the Turkish Delight Cheesecake (page 181) is a must.

Chargrilled bananas with bitter chocolate and toasted marshmallow ice cream

SERVES 4

ICE CREAM
4 large scoops of your favourite
  vanilla ice cream
8 marshmallows

BANANAS
50g caster or granulated sugar
25g unsalted butter
2 tbsp dark rum
3 under-ripe bananas, peeled
  and cut in half lengthways
1 tbsp vegetable oil

GANACHE
50g dark chocolate (minimum
  60% cocoa solids), broken
  into chunks
40ml single or double cream

GARNISH
4 large marshmallows
cocoa nibs or grated chocolate

1 Prepare the ice cream first by allowing it to soften slightly. Lightly toast the marshmallows using a blowtorch. Alternatively you can put them under the grill for 3–5 minutes. Cut them into smallish pieces and mix them into the ice cream. Put in the freezer to set.

2 For the bananas, place the sugar in a saucepan over a moderate heat and swirl until a caramel forms. Whisk in the butter and rum. Add a little water to create a thick syrup and set aside.

3 Heat a chargrill pan until it smokes. Rub the flesh of the bananas with the oil, then place them cut side down in the pan until blackened grill marks appear. Remove from the pan, cut in half and submerge in the syrup.

4 For the ganache, put the chocolate into a bowl. Bring the cream to the boil over a moderate heat, then pour it over the chocolate. Allow to sit for 2 minutes, then whisk together.

5 Preheat the oven to 180°C/350°F/gas mark 4. Arrange the pieces of banana on a baking tray and heat them gently in the oven for a couple of minutes. Place a dollop of ganache into each of the four bowls and swish up the side using a spoon. Torch or grill the garnish marshmallows until golden, then place one in each bowl. Arrange three banana pieces around a marshmallow and serve with the ice cream on the side and the cocoa nibs sprinkled on top.

Spiced rice pudding with nutmeg and plum compôte

SERVES 4–6

RICE PUDDING
400ml semi-skimmed or whole milk
100ml double cream
2 cinnamon sticks, halved
3 star anise
1 vanilla pod, seeds scraped
zest of ¼ orange
90g Arborio or Carnaroli rice
65g caster or granulated sugar
2 medium free-range egg yolks
COMPÔTE
50g caster or granulated sugar
8 ripe plums, stoned and quartered
125ml port
2 nutmegs

1 Bring the milk, cream, spices, vanilla pod (and seeds) and orange zest to the boil and boil gently for 5 minutes. Strain into a clean saucepan, then add the rice. Simmer very gently, stirring regularly, for 10–15 minutes, or until the rice is still slightly crunchy.

2 Whisk the sugar and egg yolks together and add to the rice. Stir with a spatula over a low heat until the mixture is thick enough to coat the back of a spoon and the rice is just tender. Serve immediately or chill quickly and reheat when desired.

3 For the compôte, place the sugar in a pan over a moderately high heat until the edges begin to caramelize. Swirl the pan until all the sugar has melted into a caramel.

4 Add the plums and toss around in the caramel, then deglaze with the port. Grate the nutmeg on to the plums, then allow the plums to cook for a couple of minutes until they become tender. Serve while warm along with the rice pudding.

181

Turkish delight cheesecake

SERVES 8–10

200g Rich Tea (or other plain)
    biscuits, crushed
3 tbsp cocoa powder
80g unsalted butter, plus extra
    for greasing
2 tbsp clear honey
4 leaves gelatine
250g cream cheese
25g caster sugar
250g sour cream
2 tbsp semi-skimmed or whole milk
3 × 50g bars chocolate-covered
    Turkish Delight, chopped
rosewater to taste

1 Mix together the crushed biscuits and cocoa powder. Melt the butter in a small saucepan over a moderate heat, then mix in the honey. Pour into the biscuit mixture and stir well to combine, then press into a greased springform cake tin (20cm in diameter and 8cm deep) and refrigerate.

2 Soak the gelatine leaves in a little cold water and leave in the fridge for 10 minutes. Beat the cream cheese until soft, then add the sugar and sour cream and beat well.

3 Heat the milk gently in a small saucepan, then remove from the heat. Squeeze the soaking liquid from the gelatine leaves, then add them to the milk, stirring well. Add 4 spoonfuls of the cream-cheese mixture to the milk, stir together well, then pass through a fine sieve into the remaining cream-cheese mixture. Combine well, then fold in the Turkish Delight and enough rosewater to suit your taste.

4 Blend lightly using a stick blender, or pulse briefly in a blender. Pour on to the chilled base and allow the cheesecake to set in the fridge for a couple of hours until firm.

Tiramisu doughnuts

MAKES 16

DOUGH
250g plain flour, plus extra for dusting
1 tsp fast-action dried yeast
100ml semi-skimmed or whole milk
2 medium free-range eggs
pinch table salt
50g unsalted butter, softened

SYRUP
2 tsp instant coffee
3 tbsp Marsala or coffee liqueur
100ml water
4 tbsp caster or granulated sugar

FILLING
2 tbsp icing sugar, sieved
125g mascarpone

SUGAR COATING
60g caster or granulated sugar
½ tsp instant coffee
½ tsp ground cinnamon
½ tsp cocoa powder

vegetable oil for deep frying
    and greasing

1 Place all the dough ingredients except the butter in a bowl and, using either an electric mixer with a dough hook or a wooden spoon, mix until well combined. If using a mixer, gradually add the butter, while kneading, then knead for a further 5 minutes. If using a wooden spoon, knead by hand on to a floured surface and gradually add the butter. Knead for a further 5 minutes. Place the dough in an oiled bowl, cover the bowl and put in a warm place for 20–30 minutes until doubled in volume.

2 Meanwhile, place the coffee syrup ingredients in a saucepan. Bring to a gentle boil and continue to boil, whisking well, for 5 minutes or until syrupy. Set aside to cool.

3 For the filling, beat the icing sugar into the mascarpone, then put the mixture into a piping bag, preferably with a nozzle. Mix together the sugar coating ingredients. Pass through a fine sieve into a bowl and set aside.

4 When the dough has proved, divide it into four balls, then divide each of these into four. Using the palm of your hand, roll each one in a little oil and place on a floured tray. Cover loosely with clingfilm and allow to double in volume again.

5 Heat the vegetable oil to 165°C. Deep fry the doughnuts four at a time, turning with a spoon so that they colour evenly. When golden, remove them and place on absorbent paper.

6 Preheat the oven to 200°C/400°F/gas mark 6. Put the coffee syrup into a squeezable bottle or another piping bag with a nozzle. Make a small hole in the bottom of each doughnut and squeeze in a little of the coffee syrup. Wait for a few minutes, then pipe in the mascarpone until it is just beginning to squeeze back out through the hole.

7 Heat the doughnuts in the hot oven for 30 seconds. Roll in the sugar and serve immediately.

Stilton, sherry jelly, burnt honey-baked rye crisps and candied walnuts

SERVES 4

100g Stilton

JELLY
4 leaves gelatine
250ml Pedro Ximenez sherry

CRISPS
50g unsalted butter
4 tbsp clear honey
8 thin slices rye bread

WALNUTS
100g walnuts
2 tbsp water
25g caster sugar

1 Make the jelly first. Soak the gelatine leaves in cold water for 10 minutes. Heat half the sherry in a small saucepan until it is just about to simmer. Squeeze the soaking liquid from the gelatine and add the leaves to the sherry, stirring until dissolved. Whisk well and add the remaining sherry. Pass through a fine sieve into a shallow container. Refrigerate for at least 2 hours.

2 Preheat the oven to 180°C/350°F/gas mark 4. For the crisps, melt the butter in a saucepan over a moderate heat, then whisk until it turns a golden colour and emits a nutty smell. Whisk in the honey and set aside.

3 Brush each slice of rye bread liberally with the honey butter and place on a baking tray in the oven for 5–8 minutes or until crispy.

4 Meanwhile, coat the walnuts in the water, then toss them in the sugar. Bake in the same oven for 5–7 minutes or until golden.

5 To serve, divide the Stilton, jelly, rye crisps and walnuts equally between four plates, or put them all on one large platter to share.

Raspberry eton mess

SERVES 8

MERINGUE
2 medium free-range egg whites
50g caster sugar
50g icing sugar, sieved
½ tsp freeze-dried raspberries,
   crushed
RASPBERRY CRÈME
200ml double cream
3 tbsp seedless raspberry jam
1 tbsp raspberry liqueur
½ vanilla pod, seeds scraped
FOR SERVING
1 tbsp seedless raspberry jam
1 punnet raspberries
1 tbsp raspberry liqueur
small basil leaves to garnish

1 Preheat the oven to 70°C/160°F/gas mark ¼ or lowest possible setting.

2 Whisk the egg whites until stiff peaks form, then add the caster sugar and whisk until glossy. Fold in the icing sugar, then spread the meringue thinly on a layer of baking paper or a silicon baking mat. Sprinkle with the crushed freeze-dried raspberries and place in the oven for 30 minutes.

3 Then turn the oven off and leave the meringue to sit in the oven for a further 30 minutes before removing. Break it carefully into shards and store in an airtight container.

4 For the raspberry crème, lightly whip the cream, then fold in the jam, liqueur and vanilla seeds. Whisk until stiff.

5 To assemble, put the raspberry jam into a piping bag and pipe small dots on to the plates. Place the raspberries in a bowl with the liqueur and toss gently to coat them. Divide the raspberries between the plates, laying them upside down in a small circle. Balance a shard of meringue on top of the raspberries then, using a hot spoon, form a quenelle of the raspberry crème and carefully place it on top of the meringue. Place a small shard of meringue into the quenelle and garnish with a few small basil leaves.

190

Oat-baked pears with comté

SERVES 4

100g unsalted butter
20g demerara sugar
25g golden syrup
50g rolled oats
¼ tsp ground cinnamon
2 large pears (Comice or
    Williams), peeled,
    quartered and cored
120g Comté cheese

1 Preheat the oven to 180°C/350°F/gas mark 4. Place 50g of the butter in a saucepan with the sugar and golden syrup. Heat gently until the sugar has dissolved, stirring continuously. Remove from the heat, then add the oats and cinnamon and mix well. Refrigerate.

2 Place a ball of the oat mixture on to the cored part of each pear quarter and smooth it flat.

3 Heat the remaining 50g of butter on a medium to high heat in an ovenproof frying pan just large enough to fit all the pears lying down. When the butter is foaming, add the pears and leave over the heat for 5 minutes until they begin to colour slightly.

4 Place the entire frying pan in the oven for 10 minutes, then remove the pears from the butter and allow them to cool slightly.

5 Serve the pears slightly warm, accompanied by the Comté as an unusual cheese course.

Lime meringue igloos with marinated pineapple and liquorice

MAKES 8

MERINGUE
2 medium free-range egg whites
60g caster sugar
60g icing sugar, sieved
finely grated zest of 1 lime
PINEAPPLE
½ supersweet pineapple, skin
    removed and cut into thirds
50g demerara sugar
3 star anise
4 whole black peppercorns
juice of 1 lime
IGLOOS
zest and juice of 2 limes
150ml double cream, lightly whipped
200g caster or granulated sugar
100ml water
3 medium free-range eggs, yolks
    and whites of 2 separated,
    the other left whole

½ log (1.5cm diameter) soft liquorice,
    cut in half lengthways, then into
    16 crescents

1 Make the meringue first. Preheat your oven to 70°C/160°F/gas mark ¼ or lowest possible setting. Whisk the egg whites until very stiff, then add the caster sugar and continue whisking until glossy and smooth. Fold in the icing sugar and mix until combined. Spread the meringue thinly on a sheet of greaseproof paper, sprinkle the lime zest over, and place on a baking tray in the oven for 1–2 hours or until crispy and dry. Then break the meringue into small pieces.

2 For the pineapple, cut three perfect circles out of the flesh, using a large ring-cutter (or a circle shape and a knife). Place the pineapple trim in a pan with the remaining ingredients, cover with cold water and simmer gently for 20 minutes.

3 Slice the pineapple circles thinly and place them on a shallow tray. Strain the syrup on to the sliced pineapple and refrigerate for 1 hour.

4 For the igloos, gently fold the lime zest and juice into the whipped cream. Place 100g of the sugar in a pan with 50ml of the water and bring to a rapid boil for 3 minutes. Meanwhile, slowly whisk the two egg whites to stiff peaks. Whisk the hot syrup into the stiff whites to create a glossy meringue and set aside. Make another batch of syrup using the remaining sugar and water. Combine the whole egg and two egg yolks and repeat the process with the hot syrup.

5 Carefully fold the beaten whites into the whipped cream, then fold in the yolk mixture. Spoon into eight dome moulds (or small teacups) and place in the freezer for 1–2 hours until firm.

6 Before serving, place a tray in the freezer to chill. Lay a couple of slices of pineapple on each plate. Soak the liquorice crescents in a little warm water, then arrange them on the plates. Warm the igloo moulds in your hand, then scoop out the dome parfait and place on the frozen tray. Freeze for 5 minutes, then remove and cover with the broken meringue pieces, one dome at a time, with the finished igloos going back in the freezer until all are done. Sit the igloos on the pineapple and serve immediately.

194

Gooseberry cheesecake with hobnobs

SERVES 8–10

BASE
200g Hobnob biscuits
40g unsalted butter, plus extra
    for greasing
pinch table salt
FILLING
450g gooseberries
300g caster sugar
200g crème fraîche
300g cream cheese
3 leaves gelatine
50ml semi-skimmed or whole milk
125ml lightly whipped double
    or whipping cream

1 To make the base, place the Hobnobs in a plastic bag and crush well with a rolling pin, then tip into a bowl. Melt the butter in a saucepan over a moderate heat, add the salt, then pour it over the crushed biscuits. Stir well to combine. Press down firmly into a greased springform tin (20–23cm in diameter and 8cm deep) and refrigerate.

2 For the filling, place the gooseberries and 200g of the sugar in a saucepan over a moderate heat. Stir regularly until the gooseberries are soft. Remove from the heat and refrigerate for 30 minutes.

3 Place the crème fraîche in a large bowl and whisk in the remaining sugar until smooth. Add the cream cheese and combine until smooth.

4 Soak the gelatine leaves in cold water for 3–5 minutes until just soft, then squeeze the water from the gelatine. Heat the milk until almost boiling (either in the microwave or in a saucepan), then stir in the drained gelatine.

5 Transfer one quarter of the cream-cheese mixture to another bowl and whisk in the warm milk and gelatine. Return this to the remaining cream-cheese mixture and combine well.

6 Add the chilled gooseberries to the cream-cheese mixture, then fold in the cream. Spoon on to the base and tap gently to smooth out and remove any air bubbles. Refrigerate for at least 2 hours before serving.

7 To serve, run a hot knife round the rim of the cheesecake, then release the spring and gently pop the base out of the ring. Using a palette knife, slide the cheesecake off the mould and on to a plate.

Gingerbread and butter pudding with baked pears

SERVES 6–8

1 tsp vegetable oil, for greasing
8 slices gingerbread (or ginger loaf), halved
2 large pears (Comice or Conference), peeled, cored and sliced very finely
100ml Green Ginger Wine
500ml semi-skimmed or whole milk
2 tbsp golden syrup
pinch table salt
2 medium free-range eggs
2 tsp demerara sugar
1 tsp mixed spice
50g stem ginger in syrup, finely chopped

1 Preheat the oven to 165°C/325°F/gas mark 3. Grease an ovenproof dish approximately 16cm × 16cm × 4cm.

2 Lay eight half-slices of gingerbread on the bottom of the dish, then lie half the sliced pears on top, finishing with a good splash of the ginger wine. Repeat the layering process with the rest of the gingerbread, pears and ginger wine.

3 Whisk the milk, golden syrup, salt and eggs together, then pour this over the gingerbread and pears. Mix the sugar, spice and stem ginger together and crumble over the top of the pudding.

4 Bake in the oven for 20–25 minutes until the egg mix has just set. Serve warm with crème fraîche or ice cream.

Flapjack-baked figs with crème fraîche

SERVES 4

30g demerara sugar
85g unsalted butter
40g golden syrup
85g rolled oats
½ tsp ground cinnamon,
    plus extra for sprinkling
4 large ripe, fresh figs
80g crème fraîche
icing sugar, for dusting
clear honey, for drizzling

1 Make the flapjack mixture first by placing the sugar, butter and golden syrup in a small saucepan over a moderate heat, stirring continuously until the sugar has dissolved and the mixture has combined.

2 Mix the rolled oats and cinnamon together, then pour the butter mixture over and stir until combined. Put in the fridge until required.

3 Preheat the oven to 180°C/350°F/gas mark 4. Carefully make an x-shaped incision on the top of each fig, ensuring you slice only halfway down. Stuff the incisions with half of the flapjack mixture and place the stuffed figs on a baking tray. Bake in the oven for 10 minutes.

4 Roll the remaining flapjack mixture flat between two sheets of baking paper and cook for 5–8 minutes until crispy. Leave to cool slightly, then cut into four pieces.

5 To serve, place a quenelle of the crème fraîche on each of the cooled, baked flapjacks. Dust the figs with icing sugar and serve while warm. Drizzle a little clear honey around the plate and sprinkle with ground cinnamon.

Espresso mousse with cinnamon madeleines

SERVES 6

MOUSSE
2 medium free-range eggs
150ml water
50g freshly ground espresso
125g caster or granulated sugar
250ml double or whipping cream
50ml Kahlua

MADELEINES
75g unsalted butter, plus
    extra for greasing
1 tbsp golden syrup
1 tsp ground cinnamon
¼ nutmeg, freshly grated
50g caster sugar
2 medium free-range eggs
75g plain flour

1 tsp caster sugar mixed with
    ½ tsp ground cinnamon
4 tbsp made-up espresso

1 For the mousse, place the eggs in a mixing bowl and begin to whisk at low speed. Meanwhile, bring the water to the boil, then add the coffee and simmer for 1 minute. Strain through a fine sieve into a small saucepan. Add the sugar, bring to the boil and boil rapidly for 3 minutes.

2 Continue whisking the eggs, increasing the speed to maximum, and slowly pour the hot coffee syrup down the side of the bowl on to the egg. Whisk until the bowl is cool to the touch and the egg mixture is light and fluffy.

3 Whisk the cream until soft peaks form, then fold in the Kahlua. Next, fold in the egg mixture (sabayon). Divide between six glasses or ramekins and refrigerate for at least 1 hour.

4 For the madeleines, melt the butter in a saucepan over a moderate heat then, in a bowl, mix the butter and syrup together with the spices and sugar, add the eggs and fold in the flour. Refrigerate for at least 1 hour.

5 Preheat the oven to 180°C/350°F/gas mark 4 and grease six madeleine tins with butter, then dust with the combined sugar and cinnamon. Using a piping bag, pipe the tins two thirds full with the madeleine mixture and, just before serving, bake for 8–10 minutes.

6 Serve the mousses from the fridge with the warm madeleines, spooning a little espresso over the mousses before serving.

Chocolate and cointreau self-saucing pudding

MAKES 4

PUDDINGS
100g unsalted butter, softened,
    plus extra for greasing
150g caster sugar
2 medium free-range eggs
juice and finely grated zest
    of 2 oranges
175g plain flour
2 tsp baking powder
2 tbsp cocoa powder

SAUCE
6 tbsp cocoa powder
100g soft brown sugar
400ml boiling water
30ml Cointreau

1 Preheat the oven to 180°C/350°F/gas mark 4 and grease four ramekins.

2 Cream the butter and sugar together, then add the eggs, orange juice and zest. Mix the flour, baking powder and cocoa together separately, then fold into the butter mixture. Divide the mixture evenly between the ramekins.

3 For the sauce, mix the cocoa powder and brown sugar together and sprinkle over the mixture in the ramekins.

4 Pour 100ml boiling water over the mixture in each ramekin, then place the ramekins in the oven for 10–15 minutes. Add the Cointreau evenly to the ramekins, then bake for a further 5 minutes. Serve with a large dollop of crème fraîche and vanilla ice cream.

POPCORN

The smell of popcorn permeating the cinema triggers loads of memories for everyone. Not to mention the excitement and wonderment for young and old alike of a small hard kernel of corn popping into a little fluffy white cloud.

Popcorn was first discovered thousands of years ago by the Native Americans, who believed that the popping noise was that of an angry god escaping the kernel. The 'pop' occurs because, unlike other grains, corn kernels have a hard, moisture-sealed hull and a dense, starchy filling. Heat creates a build-up of pressure inside the kernel until it effectively explodes into an edible snack.

Although popcorn is usually viewed as a treat for children, I have taken a different approach here and included recipes for all ages and tastes. Try the Pesto Popcorn (page 209) with an ice-cold beer in summer, or the Milk Chocolate and Peanut Popcorn Clusters (page 217) for a tea-time treat with friends.

204

Sesame toffee popcorn bars

MAKES 10 BARS

1 × 85g packet plain or salted
    microwave popcorn
75g sesame seeds
100g clear honey
3 tbsp sesame oil
pinch table salt

1 Line a 20cm × 15cm × 3cm baking tray with baking paper.

2 Cook the popcorn according to the manufacturer's instructions, then sort through to remove any kernels. Place the popcorn in a large mixing bowl.

3 Put the sesame seeds into a medium-sized frying pan over a moderate heat and colour until golden, then remove from the pan and set aside.

4 Heat the honey in the frying pan over a low heat, then add the sesame oil and salt and whisk well to combine. Add the sesame seeds, then pour this mixture over the popcorn and mix well with a wooden spoon.

5 Turn the popcorn on to the lined tray, spread it evenly and press down firmly, using a spatula.

6 Allow to cool and set, then turn out carefully on to a chopping board and cut into bars with a sharp, serrated knife.

Salted caramel popcorn

MAKES 1 LARGE BOWL

1 × 85g packet salted
   microwave popcorn
200g caster sugar
100g unsalted butter
½ tsp salt

1 Cook the popcorn according to the manufacturer's instructions, then sort through to remove any kernels.

2 Place the sugar in a medium-sized saucepan over a moderate heat until it begins to caramelize. Swirl the pan to ensure an even caramel, then whisk in the butter and salt.

3 When the butter and caramel combine, add the popcorn and mix well.

4 Pour the mixture on to two sheets of baking paper, pulling it apart with two forks as it cools to create individual clumps.

Sweet spiced popcorn

MAKES 1 LARGE BOWL

1 × 85g packet plain or salted
   microwave popcorn
2 tsp ground cinnamon
1 tsp ground mixed spice
¼ nutmeg, finely grated
4 tbsp icing sugar
pinch table salt
50g unsalted butter

1 Cook the popcorn according to the manufacturer's instructions, then sort through to remove any kernels.

2 Sieve all the dry ingredients together.

3 Melt the butter in a saucepan over a moderate heat. Coat the popcorn with the melted butter, then add the spice mix and toss with your hands to coat.

Popcorn and marshmallow balls

MAKES 8

1 × 85g packet plain
   microwave popcorn
4 tbsp clear honey
2 tbsp caster or granulated
   sugar
75g unsalted butter
100g marshmallows,
   cut in half

1 Cook the popcorn according to the manufacturer's instructions, then sort through to remove any kernels.

2 Place the honey, sugar and butter in a small saucepan, heat gently and stir to dissolve the sugar, then bring to the boil and boil for 2 minutes.

3 Mix the popcorn and marshmallows together, then pour the honey mixture over and mix well with a wooden spoon. Using plastic gloves, as the mixture will be hot, shape into eight balls and leave them to cool on baking paper.

Pesto popcorn

MAKES 1 LARGE BOWL

1 × 85g packet salted
   microwave popcorn
25g Parmesan, finely grated
½ bunch basil, leaves very
   finely chopped
3 tbsp pine nuts, toasted
   and finely chopped
½ tsp table salt
4 tbsp extra-virgin olive oil

1 Cook the popcorn according to the
manufacturer's instructions, then sort
through to remove any kernels.

2 Preheat the oven to 165°C/325°F/gas
mark 3. Spread the Parmesan on a baking
tray lined with baking paper. Bake for 6
minutes, then remove and chop finely.

3 Mix the chopped Parmesan with the
basil, pine nuts and salt.

4 Heat the olive oil in a saucepan over
a low heat, then pour it over the popcorn
and mix well. Add the pesto mix and toss
well to combine.

MARCUS WAREING *POPCORN*

Hot and spicy popcorn

MAKES 1 LARGE BOWL

1 × 85g packet salted microwave
    popcorn
1 tsp paprika
1 tsp curry powder
¼ tsp chilli powder
½ tsp coarsely ground black pepper
½ tsp table salt
50g unsalted butter

1 Cook the popcorn according to the manufacturer's instructions, then sort through to remove any kernels.

2 Sieve the dry ingredients together.

3 Melt the butter in a saucepan over a moderate heat. Mix the popcorn with the melted butter, then add the dry mixture and toss well to coat evenly.

Honeycomb popcorn bites

MAKES 10

1 × 85g packet plain microwave
   popcorn
3 tbsp caster or granulated sugar
3 tbsp clear honey
1 tbsp golden syrup
1 tsp bicarbonate of soda

1 Cook the popcorn according to the manufacturer's instructions, then sort through to remove any kernels.

2 Heat the sugar, honey and golden syrup in a saucepan over a moderate heat. Stir gently until the sugar has dissolved, then bring to the boil and boil for 2 minutes.

3 Remove the pan from the heat, add the bicarbonate of soda and stir quickly until the mixture foams.

4 Pour the mixture over the popcorn and mix together quickly, then pour on to baking paper, separating roughly into ten piles. Leave until cool before serving.

Parmesan and black pepper popcorn with prosciutto

MAKES 1 LARGE BOWL

1 × 85g packet salted microwave
    popcorn
50g Parmesan, finely grated
½ tsp coarsely ground black pepper
100g prosciutto, finely sliced

1 Cook the popcorn according to the manufacturer's instructions, then sort through to remove any kernels.

2 Mix the popcorn with the Parmesan, pepper and prosciutto, and toss to combine.

Honey mustard popcorn

MAKES 1 LARGE BOWL

1 × 85g packet salted microwave
    popcorn
25g unsalted butter
2 tbsp clear honey
1 tsp English mustard powder
1 tsp wholegrain mustard
½ tsp table salt
½ tsp coarsely ground black pepper

1 Cook the popcorn according to the manufacturer's instructions, then sort through to remove any kernels.

2 Put the butter and honey into a small saucepan and heat gently, whisking continuously until the mixture combines.

3 Add the mustards, salt and pepper, then pour the mixture over the popcorn and stir well to combine.

215

Crunchy nut popcorn

MAKES 1 LARGE BOWL

1 × 85g packet plain microwave
   popcorn
50g caster or granulated sugar
4 tbsp golden syrup
¼ tsp ground cinnamon
25g unsalted butter
½ tsp table salt
6 tbsp roasted peanuts,
   roughly chopped

1 Cook the popcorn according to the manufacturer's instructions, then sort through to remove any kernels.

2 Put the sugar, golden syrup and cinnamon into a medium-sized saucepan over a moderate heat until it begins to caramelize. Swirl the pan to ensure an even caramelization.

3 Whisk in the butter and salt until thoroughly combined, then quickly add the popcorn and nuts. Mix well to coat the popcorn, then spread on baking paper and break into chunks when cool.

Milk chocolate and peanut popcorn clusters

MAKES 8

1 × 85g packet plain
  microwave popcorn
2 tbsp peanut butter
6 tbsp water
50g peanuts, toasted
  and roughly chopped
100g milk chocolate,
  broken into chunks

1 Cook the popcorn according to the manufacturer's instructions, then sort through to remove any kernels.

2 Heat the peanut butter and water in a small saucepan and whisk until a smooth paste is formed, then add the chopped nuts.

3 Using your hands, mix the popcorn and the peanut paste together.

4 Melt the chocolate in a large bowl placed over a saucepan of gently simmering water. Add the melted chocolate to the popcorn and mix well.

5 Take a small handful of popcorn and form a cluster, squeezing it so that it clumps together, then place it on a tray lined with a sheet of baking paper. Repeat with the remaining mixture until you have eight clusters, then put them in the fridge for 10–20 minutes to set.

Coffee caramel popcorn chunks

MAKES 1 LARGE BOWL

1 × 85g packet plain or salted
    microwave popcorn
150g caster or granulated sugar
2 tsp instant coffee
2 tbsp boiling water
50g unsalted butter
pinch table salt

1 Cook the popcorn according to the manufacturer's instructions, then sort through to remove any kernels.

2 Place the sugar in a medium-sized frying pan over a moderate heat and melt to form a caramel. Do not stir; just swirl the pan to move the sugar around to ensure an even caramel.

3 Meanwhile, dissolve the coffee in the boiling water. When the caramel is lightly golden, whisk in the coffee and simmer for 2 minutes. Whisk in the butter until it combines to a smooth paste with the caramel. Pour the mixture over the popcorn and mix well to coat the popcorn evenly.

4 Pour on to baking paper to cool, then break up into chunks with your fingers.

Chilli and lemon popcorn

MAKES 1 LARGE BOWL

1 × 85g packet salted
    microwave popcorn
¼ tsp chilli powder
¼ tsp chilli flakes
½ tsp salt
finely grated zest of 2 lemons
4 tbsp extra-virgin olive oil

1 Cook the popcorn according to the manufacturer's instructions, then sort through to remove any kernels.

2 Mix the chilli powder, chilli flakes, salt and lemon zest together.

3 Heat the olive oil in a saucepan over a low heat, then pour it over the popcorn. Add the chilli and lemon mixture and toss well to coat the popcorn evenly.

ICE-CREAM PARLOUR

Picture this – a hot summer's day, sandy feet, a long winding queue outside the ice-cream shop. The impossible choice of selecting what flavour of ice cream, single or double scoop, cone or cup, waffle or cornet cone, choc dip or hundreds and thousands, flake or no flake . . . decisions, decisions. The first feel of cool, sweet creaminess on your tongue, then the inevitable drip rolling down your chin and plopping on to your T-shirt. Summertime and ice cream, like two peas in a pod.

In this chapter I have recreated some of my favourites, with top honours going to the Strawberry Mivi Ice Cream (page 222) – a luscious strawberry sorbet paired with a moreishly creamy milk ice cream. We serve it at the restaurant with the baked egg custard tart – a combination made in heaven. And do try the Jaffa Milkshake (page 238): it's a great chocolate–orange combination for a summer's day (even better with a splash of Cointreau for the adults).

You can make all these recipes at home without an ice-cream machine; however, they are best eaten on the day they are made to prevent them becoming icy – they don't ever last much longer than that at my house anyway!

Strawberry mivi ice cream

MAKES 1 LITRE

500g strawberries (they don't
have to be perfect ones)
100ml crème de fraises
(strawberry liqueur)
50g caster or granulated sugar
½ × 397g tin condensed milk
2 tbsp clear honey
300ml semi-skimmed or
whole milk
200ml double cream
5 medium free-range egg whites
100g caster sugar

1 Wash, hull and quarter the strawberries. Place them in a saucepan with the liqueur and the 50g sugar over a very low heat. Cook until soft, then put in a blender and blitz until smooth. Pass through a fine sieve, cover the surface with clingfilm and place in the fridge to cool.

2 Pour the condensed milk and honey into a pan and warm gently over a low heat. Remove from the heat, then whisk in the milk and cream. Cover with clingfilm and leave to cool in the fridge for 1 hour.

3 Whisk the egg whites until stiff, then slowly add the 100g caster sugar, continuing to whisk until glossy and smooth. Divide the mixture in half. Fold one half into the cooled strawberry mixture and one half into the milk mixture. Spoon each mixture into a clean plastic container, cover and place in the freezer for 2 hours.

4 When each mixture is firm enough to scoop, divide the strawberry mixture equally between two clean containers, spreading it lengthways in half of each container. Then spread the milk mixture in the other half of the container, so that it lies side by side with the strawberry mixture to form a double stripe. Cover and return to the freezer until firm.

5 Use a large spoon to scoop from the centre of the ice cream, so that each scoop has an approximately equal amount of the milk and the strawberry stripes.

1 Heat all the ingredients, except for the chocolate, in a small saucepan over a low heat until the sugar has dissolved, then simmer gently for 5 minutes, whisking continuously.

2 Put the chocolate pieces in a heatproof bowl, then pour the hot coffee mixture through a fine sieve on to the chocolate. Allow to sit for 5 minutes so that the chocolate softens, then whisk together. Serve hot or cold.

Spiced mocha sauce

SERVES 4

2 shots espresso, or 150ml very
    strong coffee
½ tsp ground cinnamon
¼ nutmeg, freshly grated
¼ tsp coarsely ground black pepper
1 star anise, grated
100ml whipping or double cream
150ml semi-skimmed or whole milk
30g caster or granulated sugar
100g dark chocolate (minimum
    60% cocoa solids), broken
    into chunks

Rocky road ice cream

MAKES 800ML

300ml semi-skimmed or whole milk
4 medium free-range eggs, yolks
   and whites separated
150g caster sugar
3 tbsp cocoa powder
2 tbsp peanut butter
300ml whipping or double cream
150g marshmallows, cut in half
100g chocolate-coated peanuts,
   cut in half
½ × 135g packet raspberry jelly,
   cut into small pieces

1 For the ice-cream base, first bring the milk to the boil, then remove it from the heat.

2 Whisk the egg yolks with 50g of the sugar, the cocoa powder and the peanut butter, then whisk in a little of the hot milk.

3 Add this mixture to the rest of the hot milk in the saucepan and stir over a low heat until the mixture is thick enough to coat the back of a spoon.

4 Remove from the heat and stir in 100ml of the cream, then pour through a fine sieve into a shallow container. Cover the surface of the mixture with clingfilm to prevent a skin from forming and refrigerate for roughly 1 hour until cold.

5 Whip the remaining 200ml of cream until it stands in soft peaks, then set aside. Whisk the egg whites until stiff peaks form, then add the remaining 100g sugar and whisk further until you have a smooth and glossy meringue.

6 Fold the ice-cream base and whipped cream together, then fold in the marshmallows, peanuts and jelly pieces so that they are evenly distributed. Fold in one quarter of the meringue, then add the remaining meringue and mix gently.

7 Transfer the mixture to a suitable container for your freezer and cover with a well-fitting lid. Freeze until firm enough to scoop – 2–4 hours.

226

Marshmallow, chocolate and vanilla ice-cream sandwiches

MAKES 4

50g milk chocolate, broken
    into chunks
8 ice-cream wafers
16 marshmallows
4 large scoops vanilla ice cream

1 Melt the chocolate in a bowl placed over a small pan of simmering water. Remove from the heat, then spread the melted chocolate on to one side of four of the wafers and place them in the fridge for 10 minutes to set.

2 Place the marshmallows in a bowl in the microwave on high for 1 minute, or in a small bowl placed over rolling boiling water for about 5 minutes, until they have melted.

3 Spread the melted marshmallows evenly on to one side of the other four wafers. Put all eight wafers into the freezer for 15 minutes or until firm.

4 Remove from the freezer and spread the ice cream on to the chocolate wafers, then sandwich these together with the marshmallow wafers. Smooth the edges with a knife, then store in the freezer until ready to serve. It's best to eat these within 24 hours.

Raspberry and chocolate soda crush

MAKES 4 LARGE GLASSES

200g fresh or frozen raspberries
100g icing sugar
4 large scoops chocolate ice cream
600ml soda water
200ml lemonade
½ × 50g chocolate flake bar,
    crumbled

1 Mix the raspberries and icing sugar together, slightly crushing some of the raspberries (if they are not very sweet you may need to add more sugar).

2 Place four glasses in the freezer for 5 minutes. When you take them out, divide the raspberries evenly between each glass and add a scoop of ice cream. Combine the soda water and lemonade in a large jug and use it to top up each glass, mixing well to distribute the raspberry flavour.

3 Sprinkle crumbled chocolate flake on top of each glass, then serve immediately with a tall sundae spoon and a straw.

Passionfruit and vanilla soda float

MAKES 4 LARGE GLASSES

juice of 2 limes and finely grated
zest of 1
4 passionfruit, halved, deseeded
and pulp scraped out
4 large scoops vanilla ice cream
800ml lemonade

1 Place four glasses in the freezer for 5 minutes.

2 Mix the lime juice and zest with the passionfruit pulp, then divide the mixture evenly between the four glasses.

3 Put a scoop of ice cream in each glass, then top them up with the lemonade and serve immediately.

Marmalade and cointreau drizzle

SERVES 6–8

500ml freshly squeezed orange
    juice (roughly 4 oranges)
100g orange marmalade
50ml Cointreau

1 In a pan bring the orange juice to a gentle simmer and reduce by half.

2 Remove from the heat, add the remaining ingredients and stir well. Blend together to form a smooth sauce. Serve warm or cold.

Ice-cream cones

MAKES 12

50g unsalted butter, plus extra
    for greasing
2 medium free-range eggs
½ vanilla pod, seeds scraped,
    or ½ tsp vanilla extract
100g caster sugar
50g plain flour

1 Melt the butter in a small saucepan over a moderate heat. Place the eggs, vanilla seeds and sugar in a bowl, pour in the melted butter and mix well until combined. Add the flour and mix until smooth. Refrigerate for 1 hour until firm.

2 Preheat the oven to 165°C/325°F/gas mark 3.

3 Line a baking tray with baking paper, grease lightly and spread a small teaspoonful of the mixture at a time on to the baking paper in semicircle shapes (you may find this easier if you make a template out of an old ice-cream container lid). You should have enough mixture for about 12 semicircles. Bake in the oven for 3–5 minutes or until barely golden.

4 Remove from the oven, cool for a few seconds on the tray, then roll the semicircles into cone shapes, using a hornet cone mould if available, reheating a little if necessary. Remove when cooled (after roughly 30 seconds) and store in an airtight container for up to 3 days.

Liquorice allsort ice cream

MAKES 1 LITRE

300ml semi-skimmed or whole milk
7 medium free-range egg yolks,
    plus 3 whites
200g caster sugar
300ml whipping or double cream
2 tbsp Sambuca
½ × 215g packet Liquorice Allsorts,
    chopped into quarters
mini Liquorice Allsorts to garnish

1 Bring the milk to the boil in a saucepan, then remove from the heat.

2 In a small bowl, whisk the egg yolks with 100g of the sugar, then whisk in a little of the hot milk. Add this mixture to the hot milk in the saucepan and stir over a low heat until it is thick enough to coat the back of a spoon.

3 Add 100ml of the cream and the Sambuca, then pour through a fine sieve into a shallow container. Cover the surface of the ice-cream base with clingfilm to prevent a skin from forming and refrigerate for 1 hour until cold.

4 Whip the remaining 200ml of cream to soft peaks. In a separate bowl, whisk the egg whites until stiff peaks form, then add the remaining 100g sugar and whisk further until you have a smooth and glossy meringue.

5 Fold the ice-cream base and whipped cream together, then fold in the chopped Liquorice Allsorts, making sure they are evenly distributed. Fold in one quarter of the meringue, then add the remaining meringue and mix gently together until combined.

6 Transfer the mixture to a suitable container for your freezer and cover with a well-fitting lid. Freeze until firm enough to scoop (2–4 hours).

7 Sprinkle the mini Liquorice Allsorts over the ice cream before serving.

1 Combine the lemon juice, zest and sugar in a small saucepan. Add the water and heat until the sugar has dissolved, stirring continuously. Pour into a shallow container in the fridge for 1 hour so that the syrup cools quickly.

2 Chill the four serving glasses in the freezer for 5 minutes.

3 Transfer the cold lemon syrup to a large jug and add the soda water.

4 With a sharp knife, finely chop the mint leaves. Remove the glasses from the freezer and add one scoop of ice cream and some of the mint to each one. Pour the lemonade over the ice cream and serve immediately with a long straw.

234

Home-made lemonade and vanilla ice-cream soda float

MAKES 4 LARGE GLASSES

juice of 3 lemons and finely grated
    zest of 1
200g caster or granulated sugar
50ml water
1 litre soda water
4 large scoops vanilla ice cream
8–12 mint leaves

Gin and tonic granité

MAKES 1 LITRE

200g caster or granulated sugar
100ml water
250ml good-quality gin
    (Bombay Sapphire or Beefeater)
juice of 2 lemons
500ml tonic water
crystallized violet petals
    to garnish (optional)

1 In a small saucepan, heat the sugar with the water over a low heat until the sugar dissolves, stirring continuously. Put the gin, lemon juice and tonic water in a bowl and pour the water and sugar mixture over. Transfer to a suitable container for your freezer. Leave to freeze for 2 hours, whisking after the first and second hour.

2 Before serving, scrape with a fork to break up the granité to give it a softer texture. Serve with crystallized violet petals as a pre-dessert or summer's day adult slushy!

Christmas pudding and custard ice cream

MAKES 1 LITRE

500g custard (store-bought or
   home-made)
300ml double or whipping cream,
   whipped to form soft peaks
150g cooked Christmas pudding
generous splash brandy
3 medium free-range egg whites
75g caster sugar

1 Gently mix the custard and whipped cream together in a large mixing bowl. In another bowl, break up the Christmas pudding with your fingers and splash it liberally with brandy before adding it to the custard mixture.

2 Place the egg whites into a mixing bowl and, using an electric mixer or a hand-held electric mixer, whisk until stiff peaks form. Slowly add the sugar while still whisking, and beat until you have a glossy and firm meringue.

3 Fold the meringue gently into the custard mixture, then pour into a suitable container, lay clingfilm directly over the surface to prevent a skin forming and place in the freezer for a minimum of 2 hours before serving.

237

Banana caramel sauce

SERVES 6–8

200g caster or granulated sugar
2 over-ripe bananas, mashed
50ml banana liqueur (optional)
pinch table salt
150g crème fraîche

1 Place the sugar in a pan over a moderately high heat until the edges begin to caramelize. Swirl the pan to distribute the sugar evenly until it has all melted into a caramel.

2 Add the mashed banana, liqueur (if using) and salt, and mix well. Cook over a low heat, stirring continuously, until the caramel has melted back into the banana – this will take 10–15 minutes.

3 Add the crème fraîche, mix well and remove from the heat. Blend, using a stick blender or large blender, and pass through a fine sieve. Serve hot or cold.

1 Put all the ingredients, except for the chocolate flake, into a blender and blend until smooth.

2 Pour the mixture into ice-cold glasses and sprinkle with the crumbled flake bar. Serve immediately.

Jaffa milkshake

**MAKES 4 SMALL
OR 2 LARGE GLASSES**

600ml ice-cold semi-skimmed
   or whole milk
2 scoops chocolate ice cream
small handful ice cubes
2 tbsp drinking-chocolate powder
juice of 1 orange
3 tbsp orange marmalade
50ml Cointreau (optional)
1 × 50g chocolate flake bar,
   crumbled

Honeycomb milkshake

MAKES 4 SMALL OR 2 LARGE GLASSES

2 tbsp golden syrup
1 tbsp clear honey
1 litre semi-skimmed or whole milk
2 scoops vanilla ice cream
2 × 50g Crunchie bars, crumbled

1 Put the golden syrup, honey and milk in the bowl of a blender and whisk, then add the ice cream and blend until smooth. Add half the crumbled Crunchie bars and pulse twice to disperse.

2 Pour the mixture into glasses and sprinkle with the remaining crumbled Crunchie bars. Serve immediately.

Cola jelly with vanilla ice cream

MAKES 4 MEDIUM
(300 ML) GLASSES

10 leaves gelatine
2 × 330ml cans cola
4 large scoops vanilla ice cream
approximately 20 sour cola-bottle
    sweets, cut into quarters

1 Cover the gelatine leaves in cold water and soak until soft.

2 Heat 100ml of the cola in a small saucepan but do not allow to boil. Squeeze the soaking liquid out of the gelatine leaves, add them to the cola and stir until dissolved. Mix in the remaining cola, then pass through a fine sieve.

3 Pour evenly into four glasses and refrigerate for a minimum of 2 hours.

4 To serve, place a scoop of ice cream on top of each of the set jellies and sprinkle with the chopped cola-bottle sweets.

SWEET SHOP

The will-power to walk past a sweet shop is not something I possess – rows upon rows of jars, each containing yet another sweetly satisfying morsel! Sweet shops have such a nostalgic atmosphere when you walk in, with a warming smell and sight unlike any other to trigger those wonderful childhood memories.

Sweets I enjoyed as a boy continue to be the ones I can't pass up now – Turkish Delight, Chocolate-covered Honeycomb and Chocolate Éclair Bonbons, to name a few. I have therefore included these in this chapter (pages 244, 249 and 254) so that you can make them for yourselves at home.

I also love giving friends and family home-made sweets instead of buying the classic box of chocolates. We make our own chocolate bonbons at the restaurant and serve them from an ornate trolley with hanging baskets for guests to complete their meal. Currently we have peanut butter and jelly chocolates rolled in a crunchy sweet crumb – a bit like peanut butter and jelly on toast – which are fantastic. An old favourite is also salted caramel, which many people cannot resist. However, Turkish Delight is my definite favourite.

Turkish delight

SERVES 10

juice of 1 lemon
550g caster or granulated sugar
45ml rosewater
125ml water
drop of pink food colouring
65g cornflour
15 leaves gelatine
100g milk chocolate, broken
    into chunks

1 Line a small 10cm × 7cm × 5cm tin with clingfilm.

2 Place all the ingredients, except the gelatine and chocolate, into a saucepan, bring to a gentle simmer and continue simmering for 15 minutes.

3 Soak the gelatine leaves in cold water until soft. Squeeze the soaking mixture from the gelatine, then whisk the leaves into the hot mixture. Pour into the tin and refrigerate for 1 hour until firm.

4 Melt the chocolate in a bowl placed over a saucepan of simmering water. Remove the Turkish Delight from the tin and peel off the clingfilm. Cover all the sides liberally with the melted chocolate, put it on a small sheet of baking paper and then refrigerate. Slice when the chocolate is set and store in the fridge for up to 1 week.

Orange sherbet with liquorice dippers

MAKES 8

finely grated zest of 2 oranges
200g granulated sugar
½ tsp bicarbonate of soda
½ tsp citric acid
8 liquorice sticks

1 Preheat the oven to 60°C/140°F/gas mark ¼ or lowest possible setting.

2 Mix the orange zest with the sugar, then spread it on to baking paper on a baking tray and place in the oven for 30 minutes or until the sugar has dried.

3 Mix the bicarbonate of soda, citric acid and orange sugar together and push through a sieve. Serve in eight small bowls or shot glasses with liquorice sticks to dip in.

Marshmallow biscuit bonbons

MAKES 40

200g unsalted butter
1 × 397g tin condensed milk
125g soft brown sugar
2 tbsp cocoa powder
1 × 300g packet Rich Tea (or similar)
    biscuits, crushed
1 × 200g packet marshmallows,
    each cut in half
desiccated coconut, toasted

1 Place the butter, condensed milk, sugar and cocoa powder in a saucepan over a moderate heat. Stir until combined and the mixture is beginning to bubble. Pour into a large bowl with the biscuit crumbs and mix well.

2 Take a small spoonful of the biscuit mix and shape it around a marshmallow piece. Roll it into a ball shape, then roll in the coconut. Store in the fridge.

White chocolate and raspberry coconut ice

MAKES 32 PIECES

600g icing sugar, sieved
1 × 397g tin condensed milk
100ml semi-skimmed or whole milk
25g unsalted butter
pinch table salt
200g desiccated coconut
100g white chocolate
4 tbsp raspberry jam

1 Place the icing sugar, condensed milk, milk, butter and salt in a medium-sized saucepan. Heat gently, stirring until the sugar has dissolved. Bring to a gentle boil and continue boiling until the mixture reaches soft-ball stage (when a little is dropped into cold water and forms a soft ball).

2 Add the coconut, then remove from the heat and allow to cool slightly. Divide the mixture in two. Add the white chocolate to one part and beat until it thickens. Pour into a greased cake tin, approximately 30cm × 15cm × 3cm, and refrigerate until firm to the touch (around 20 minutes).

3 Beat the raspberry jam into the remaining mixture until it thickens, then spread this on top of the chocolate mixture in the tin. Allow to set in the fridge for 30–40 minutes, then cut into squares.

249

Chocolate-covered honeycomb

MAKES ABOUT 20 PIECES

150g caster or granulated sugar
3 tbsp clear honey
1 tbsp golden syrup
2 tsp bicarbonate of soda
100g milk chocolate, broken
   into chunks

1 Put the sugar, honey and golden syrup into a saucepan and heat gently until the sugar dissolves, stirring occasionally. Increase the heat and boil rapidly for 3 minutes.

2 Remove from the heat, stir in the bicarbonate of soda and quickly pour on to a baking tray lined with baking paper. Leave to cool for 15 minutes, then break into chunks and arrange on baking paper.

3 Melt the chocolate in a bowl placed over a pan of simmering water. Using a dipping swirl or a fork, dip the pieces of honeycomb into the chocolate, shake off the excess, then place them carefully back on the baking paper to set. Refrigerate and consume the same day, or freeze for up to 2 weeks to prevent the honeycomb softening.

Rice crispie squares

MAKES 20

4 tbsp caster sugar
2 tbsp clear honey
125g unsalted butter
150g Rice Crispies

1 Grease a 27.5cm × 17.5cm baking tray with an edge.

2 Place the sugar, honey and butter in a saucepan and bring to a gentle simmer until it has lightly coloured, stirring occasionally.

3 Pour the warm mixture over the Rice Crispies, mix well, then press into the baking tray. Leave for 10 minutes, then cut into squares.

Decadent hot chocolate

SERVES 2

400ml semi-skimmed milk
pinch chilli flakes
¼ tsp cinnamon
100g dark chocolate (minimum
    60% cocoa solids), chopped
    into pieces
2 tbsp brandy
6 marshmallows
½ × 50g chocolate flake bar

1 Half fill two large glasses with boiling water and allow to sit.

2 Place the milk, chilli and cinnamon into a medium-sized saucepan and bring to a gentle simmer.

3 Empty the water out of the glasses and divide the pieces of chocolate between them.

4 Add the brandy to the milk, then strain through a tea strainer into the glasses. Add 3 marshmallows to each glass and crumble the chocolate flake over the top. Serve with two long spoons, one per glass.

Peppermint cream chocolate truffles

MAKES 24

65g cream cheese
200g icing sugar, sieved
peppermint essence, to taste
100g dark chocolate (minimum
    60% cocoa solids), broken
    into chunks
3 packets extra-strong mints,
    finely crushed

1 Mix the cream cheese, icing sugar and peppermint essence together until smooth. Put in the fridge to set for 1 hour. Roll into small balls and return to the fridge.

2 Melt the chocolate in a bowl placed over a small saucepan of simmering water.

3 Place the crushed mints into a shallow, wide dish. Using a dipping swirl or a slotted spoon, dip the mint balls into the chocolate until completely covered.

4 Swirl the excess chocolate off and tip the balls into the mint crunch. Shake the dish to coat the balls, then place them in a container while you finish the rest. Store the truffles in the fridge for up to two weeks.

Chocolate éclair bonbons

MAKES 24

GANACHE
40ml whipping or double cream
75g dark chocolate (minimum
    60% cocoa solids), broken
    into pieces
25g unsalted butter

CARAMEL
50g caster or granulated sugar
1 tbsp golden syrup
25g unsalted butter, plus extra
    for greasing
1 × 397g tin condensed milk

1 Make the ganache first. Bring the cream to the boil and pour it over the chocolate and butter. Allow to sit for a few minutes, then whisk well. Leave to cool.

2 For the caramel, grease a piece of baking paper and lay it on a flat surface. Place all the ingredients in a medium-sized saucepan over a low to moderate heat. Heat gently, stirring continuously, until the sugar has dissolved. Continue to cook over a low heat and keep stirring until the mixture becomes very thick. Pour it on to the paper and allow to cool completely.

3 Place the caramel on a chopping board, slice it in half and trim the edges. Smear half of the chocolate ganache on to each caramel rectangle, leaving a 2cm gap at the end. Roll the caramel into two tight spirals, then cover in clingfilm and refrigerate for 30 minutes.

4 Using a sharp knife run under hot water, cut each roll into 1cm slices. Wrap in candy paper or cellophane and twist at each end. Store in the fridge for up to 1 week.

Black forest fudge

MAKES 25 PIECES

250g caster or granulated sugar
50g unsalted butter, plus extra
    for greasing
100ml double or whipping cream
100ml semi-skimmed or whole milk
100g dark chocolate (minimum
    60% cocoa solids), broken
    into chunks
100g dried sour cherries

1 Put all the ingredients, except the chocolate and sour cherries, into a medium-sized saucepan over a moderate heat. Stir constantly until the sugar has dissolved, then bring to a gentle boil and simmer for 15 minutes. Do not stir.

2 When the mixture reaches the soft-ball stage (when a little is dropped into cold water and forms a soft ball), remove it from the heat. Allow it to stand for 5 minutes, then beat with an electric beater until thick.

3 Fold in the chocolate and sour cherries and place the mixture in a greased cake tin (approximately 15cm × 15cm × 5cm) and transfer to the fridge to set for 30–40 minutes. Cut into squares when cooled.

Almond and honey marshmallows

MAKES 25 PIECES

75g flaked almonds, toasted
12 leaves gelatine
150g caster or granulated sugar
7 tbsp clear honey
100ml water
2 medium free-range egg whites

1 Line a wet cake tin (approximately 15cm × 15cm × 5cm) with clingfilm, pressing firmly into the corners. Finely chop 50g of the toasted almonds and place half in the lined container.

2 Soak the gelatine leaves in cold water until soft, then squeeze out the water and keep the gelatine in the fridge.

3 Put the sugar, honey and water into a saucepan over a moderate heat and bring to the boil. Add the gelatine and stir until dissolved, then boil steadily for 4 minutes. Meanwhile, whisk the egg whites on high speed until thick, then pour in the boiling syrup and continue to whisk until the mixture is thick and fluffy.

4 Fold in the 25g flaked almonds, then scrape the mixture into the tin and smooth the top with wet hands.

5 Sprinkle with the remaining chopped toasted almonds, then refrigerate for 1 hour. Cut into squares using a wet knife.

260

Creamy caramel fudge

MAKES 25 PIECES

700g caster or granulated sugar
125ml semi-skimmed or whole milk
½ × 397g tin condensed milk
125g unsalted butter, plus extra
    for greasing
pinch table salt
1 tbsp golden syrup

1 Put the sugar and milk in a saucepan over a low heat, stirring continuously, until the sugar dissolves. Add the remaining ingredients and bring to a gentle boil, without stirring, until the mixture reaches soft-ball stage (when a little is dropped into cold water and forms a soft ball).

2 Remove from the heat and allow to cool slightly, then beat with an electric mixer until thick (5–10 minutes). Pour into a greased cake tin (approximately 15cm × 15cm × 5cm), leave to cool, then cut into squares.

Chocolate crackle cakes

MAKES 24

100g dark chocolate (minimum
    60% cocoa solids), broken
    into pieces
75g unsalted butter, plus extra
    for greasing
pinch table salt
150g cornflakes
50g flaked almonds, toasted
25g desiccated coconut, toasted
75g icing sugar, plus extra
    for dusting
4 tbsp cocoa powder

1 Place the chocolate, butter and salt in a bowl placed over a pan of simmering water until completely melted.

2 Mix the cornflakes, almonds and coconut together in a large bowl.

3 Sieve the icing sugar and cocoa powder together and mix into the melted chocolate.

4 Pour the chocolate mixture over the cornflake mixture and gently mix together. Form rough balls with your hands and place on a tray lined with lightly greased baking paper. Refrigerate for 30 minutes until set, then dust with icing sugar just before serving.